NEW ORLEANS
A Photographic Journey

TEXT: **Suzi Forbes**

CAPTIONS: **Fleur Robertson**

DESIGNED BY: **Teddy Hartshorn**

EDITORIAL: **Gill Waugh and Jane Adams**

PRODUCTION: **Ruth Arthur, David Proffit and Sally Connolly**

DIRECTOR OF PRODUCTION: **Gerald Hughes**

DIRECTOR OF PUBLISHING: **David Gibbon**

CLB 2453
© 1990 Colour Library Books Ltd., Godalming, Surrey, England.
All rights reserved.
This 1990 edition published by Crescent Books,
distributed by Outlet Book Company, Inc., a Random House Company
225 Park Avenue South, New York, New York 10003.
Printed and bound in Hong Kong.
ISBN 0 517 01498 X
8 7 6 5 4 3 2 1

NEW ORLEANS

A Photographic Journey

Text by
SUZI FORBES

CRESCENT BOOKS

NEW YORK

Are you looking for a little something extra? A special extra something that you know you do not really deserve? In New Orleans they have a name for it. In Creole they call it *lagniappe* – "something extra," an additional, unprescribed measure, found often where least expected.

Moreover, New Orleans has a great deal of charm perhaps brought about by its long history and famous lace-like, wrought-iron balconies surrounding town houses in one of the most fascinating neighborhoods of any city in the United States: the Vieux Carré, or "Old French Quarter." It contains over 554,000 people who might say "hello" in either French, Spanish, Cajun or English. It all adds up to an enormous amount of something extra – *lagniappe*.

New Orleans is also the only major city in the United States that lies under sea level, and it has a greater annual rainfall – fifty-nine inches a year – than any other U.S. city except Miami and Mobile. Furthermore, it is washed by the mightiest river in the United States, the Mississippi. At its back door lies Lake Pontchartrain, the tenth largest lake in the United States, covering 625 square miles. If one counts all the little islands offshore, Louisiana has more shoreline than any other state except Florida and Alaska.

With all that water, one might think the city would have been washed away. In fact, the first French settlers did dub this piece of dry land squeezed between two giant bodies of water *Le Flottant* – "The Floating Land." The English, more fatalistically, named it the "Wet Grave."

At one time, many years ago, the entire state of Louisiana was under water, but as the river advanced, the sea retreated, leaving behind a baffling complex of lakes, bayous, marshes, swamps, bays, islands, estuaries and tributaries. An early French explorer called it "an impossible place, fit only for the jungle savage and the prehistoric crocodile." Even today, the swamps and marshes are home to thousands of alligators. They were also the perfect hiding places for privateers and smugglers. For example, the famous pirate, Jean Lafitte, used Barataria Bay as his home base and called it his "back door to New Orleans."

There is evidence that nomadic Indians fished the bayous and tilled the swampland for at least 10,000 years before the first Europeans arrived. They learned to adapt themselves to this sluggish, humid land and they followed the river as it flowed and overflowed, changed course and returned to its original banks. They lived abundantly on shrimp, crab, fish and oysters. They were peaceful, amiable folk who never wandered far from their big river.

They named this giant river *Mississippi*, meaning "Father of Waters" and the name persisted, despite subsequent Spanish, French (who tried to rename it the St. Louis) and English colonies.

Choctaw Indians probably greeted the first European settlers. Most accounts say that Luis de Moscoso, one of the bedraggled survivors of De Soto's expedition, was the first to sail down the Mississippi past present-day New Orleans. That was in 1543. However, he did not stop and he made no claim to the land for Spain.

The Indians were not to see another ship, or even an explorer, for almost 150 years, so those who might have spotted de Moscoso's boat must have been thought to be mad. Perhaps even any possible legends had died by the time the French arrived. The French had been active in Quebec for some time, establishing fur-trading outposts and exporting goods from them to France. It was from these outposts that the more adventurous set out to explore the interior. As they pushed southwestward they discovered Lake Michigan and then Lake Winnebago. That led them to the Wisconsin River and finally to the headwaters of the Mississippi. Now this really was a great river. They thought at first that it led to the Gulf of California, and they called it the "Vermilion Sea" because of its reddish color.

Finally, in 1682, René-Robert Cavelier, Sieur de La Salle, on an expedition for Louis XIV of France, sailed down the Mississippi River, this time from the Illinois River with a band of fifty-six settlers. La Salle was thirty-nine years old when he planted the French flag in Louisiana and named the new French acquisition "Louisiane" for his benefactor.

King Louis was very pleased. Land meant power and he certainly did not want the Spanish to have more power than he had, and he wanted a fortified colony at the mouth of this great river. So he supplied La Salle with four mighty ships and about 400 men to accomplish it.

Unfortunately this expedition turned out to be one of the more disastrous in history. The main supply ship was captured by the Spanish before it even reached the Indies. La Salle and his naval commander, Beaujeu, never had an untroubled relationship and, confined to close quarters on board ship, their enmity grew. In fact, relations deteriorated to such an extent that they argued their way right past the mouth of the Mississippi and eventually landed 500 miles west of their goal in Matagorda Bay, now a part of Texas. Here, one ship was lost in a tropical storm and another ran aground. Then, in a final pique, Beaujeu took the remaining ship and sailed back to France.

That left La Salle stranded with only forty-five discontented men and no supplies. Undaunted, he built a fort which he named St. Louis and tried fruitlessly for two years to find the Mississippi, without success. Finally, he split up his men, leaving half behind to "hold the fort." He set off with the other half to attempt to reach Quebec, but only a few miles from Fort St. Louis at the Brazos River, he was ambushed and killed by his mutinous men. The remains of his settlement were never found. This left Louis XIV with the distinction of having claimed a vast new territory called "Louisiane," but having there no settlements, no trading posts and no one to defend it. Said he: "Exploration without occupation means nothing!" That became a particular problem for France when Spain claimed all the territory on the Gulf of Mexico. Clearly, it was time for another expedition from France. This time, and by now it was 1699, the "Sun King" sent four ships, one hundred soldiers and about 200 settlers, under the command of the brothers Pierre Le Moyne, Sieur d'Iberville, and Jean Baptiste Le Moyne, Sieur de Bienville.

These dashing, rich adventurers had been raised in Quebec and were used to the rigors of frontier life. They sailed from France via St. Domingue and landed near the site of present-day Biloxi, Mississippi. Realizing that they were close to the elusive mouth of the great river, the brothers lost no time in setting out by themselves in a small boat to find it. They had to overcome a storm, unleashing gale-force winds, driving rain, thunder and lightning; and they ran into logs, snags, silt ledges and swirling, rock-infested waters before they finally passed *Malbouche*, "The Bad Mouth," and set up camp near a bayou. It was the night of Mardi Gras, 1699. Never losing their love of homeland or their sense of humor, they held the first Mardi Gras in the new land, naming the bayou *Mardi Gras Bayou* and the spit of land *Pointe de Mardi Gras*.

Iberville was thirty-eight years old and devoted to his King. He could scarcely wait to return to France and share this wonderful discovery with the court. Bienville, a young man of twenty, elected to remain in Louisiana to look after the new fort at Biloxi. As it turned out, Iberville returned twice more, but died of yellow fever in Havana Bay on his third trip.

By that time, Bienville was twenty-six years old and held the title of Governor of Louisiana. He was a veteran of life on the bayous, but he was beset with problems. No one could get used to the poor soil in Biloxi, so he moved the fort east to Mobile Bay. Indians there taught them to use corn and to grow other native crops. Nevertheless, they missed French food and wine.

None of Bienville's colony had liked Biloxi, but they were no better pleased with Mobile. Dissent and general unhappiness was the mood of the day. New settlers came expecting to find gold and silver and there was none. Furthermore, many settlers were recruited from the jails of France. They were not perhaps the best candidates for settlement. They were not farmers and they did not plant the fields. With no crops, there was no food.

Finally, in 1712, Bienville was replaced as governor by a tough merchant, Antoine Cadillac, the future founder of Detroit. Cadillac had made his fortune in the slave trade and had no time for dissenters. He was insulting and imperious and thoroughly disliked.

Cadillac wrote back to France: "The inhabitants are no better than the country; they are the very scum and refuse of Canada, ruffians who have thus far cheated the gibbet of its due, vagabonds who are without subordination to the laws, without any respect for religion or for the government, graceless profligates, who are so steeped in vice that they prefer the Indian females to the French women. Believe me, this whole continent is not worth having, and our colonists are so dissatisfied that they are all disposed to run away."

Cadillac did not last long. Bienville was elevated to the position of governor once more.

At this point John Law, a flamboyant, irascible Scot, who was ousted from England after killing a man in a duel appeared on the scene. He had been roaming Europe for fifteen years and was now living in Paris. Law was the ultimate financial schemer and gambler. Familiar with the French court, he saw Louisiana as a ripe land just waiting to be exploited. He proposed combining the Royal Bank with a giant land-speculation company to form "The Company of the West."

Public Relations was John Law's forté. He had giant posters printed, extolling the virtues of this French outpost, painting vivid pictures of a paradise on earth. The posters showed lovely Indian maidens, breasts exposed, greeting new settlers with handfuls of gold and silver. Moreover, he talked about mountains of diamonds, pearls and emeralds. He circulated maps showing attractive houses on tree-lined streets in existing cities. He promised that the gigantic French debt would be erased.

Adventurous though Louis XIV might have been, he was contentious too. His endless wars had plunged France into hopeless debt and his explorations had not yielded the immense wealth he had hoped for. In fact, they had constituted another enormous drain on the French budget. However, Louis XIV died in 1715, leaving his five-year-old grandson as Head of State. This made matters worse because, as regent until the boy's majority, France was encumbered with Philippe, Louis XIV's dissolute son-in-law. This was good for John Law. Philippe approved his scheme and granted The Company of the West a monopoly on all French trade with Asia, Africa and America and made it virtually the exclusive owner of the entire Mississippi Valley.

Law convinced everyone, from the French nobility to the common farmer, to invest in his new land scheme. Canadians, Africans, Germans, residents of the West Indies, as well as Frenchmen mortgaged their homes to buy his stock. Others took the ships he provided to seek their fortunes as homesteaders, miners or prospectors.

Even though word regularly reached France that Louisiana's soil was poor, that there was no gold, that there were quantities of alligators and mosquitoes and that Louisiana was blanketed in damp, fetid air, John Law overcame all objections – with less than entire honesty. However, his scheme did have one brilliant result: the foundation of New Orleans city.

Bienville had been looking for the perfect spot on which to build his ideal city ever since he arrived, and eventually he had found it in a "beautiful crescent of the river." It was 110 miles above the mouth of the river, so it would avoid many of the worst storms and hurricanes, and it was only five miles from lovely Lake Pontchartrain. Even though he had received no approval from France to build the French capital in this location, Bienville started construction. One of the settlers wrote to France that the village was "situated in flat and swampy ground fit only for growing rice; river water filters through under the soil and crayfish abound so that tobacco and vegetables are hard to raise. There are frequent fogs and, the land being thickly wooded and covered with canebrakes, the air is fever-laden, and an infinity of mosquitoes cause further inconvenience in summer." Nevertheless, awful as it sounded, Bienville was not ordered to give up his dream. In fact, in October 1718, John Law and his Company of the West gave formal approval to the new city, and thus the city of New Orleans was founded.

It is hard to imagine the difficulties encountered by Bienville in the beginning. John Law promoted New Orleans as we see it today, and he had some measure of success. Ironically enough, his greatest success came with the Germans not the French. A group of German families settled about thirty miles upriver from New Orleans and prospered greatly. The area has ever since been known alternately as the German Coast and the Gold Coast, where German industry and diligence made it a fine example for others to follow.

It was a German settler who perhaps gave the first account of New Orleans, the city: "I betook myself to where they are beginning the capital, New Orleans. Its circumference is one mile. The houses are poor and low, as with us at home in the country. They are covered with bark and reeds. Everyone dresses as he pleases, but all very poorly. One's outfit consists of a suit of clothes, bed, table and trunk. The people sleep the whole night in the open air. I am as safe in the more distant part of town as in a citadel. Although I live among savages and the Frenchmen, I am in no danger. People trust one another so much that they leave the gates and doors open."

Father Pierre François-Xavier de Charlevoix had read John Law's descriptions. He arrived in 1721 and wrote: "The eight-hundred beautiful houses in the five parishes which *Le Mercure* described two years ago are limited to a hundred huts placed without much order; to a large store built of wood; to two or three houses which would not adorn a French village; to the half of a wretched warehouse which the people willingly lent to the Lord and of which He had barely taken possession before they wanted to drive Him forth to lodge Him in a tent."

Even with all his potent salesmanship could do, John Law was having trouble persuading honest, hard-working people to emigrate to Louisiana. They bought his stock, but making the move was another matter altogether. Seldom daunted, he appealed to Philippe. The regent's response was perhaps unhelpful. He emptied the jails and rounded up dissenters and the homeless for repatriation in the new land. What better chance to rid France of its undesirables?. In the words of a Louisiana historian: "The [French] government went boldly to the task of ransacking the jails and hospitals. Disorderly soldiers, black sheep of distinguished families, paupers, prostitutes, political suspects, friendless strangers, unsophisticated peasants straying into Paris, all were kidnapped, herded, and shipped under guard to fill the emptiness of Louisiana. To those who would emigrate voluntarily the Company offered free land, free provisions, free transportation to the colony and from the colony to the situation of their grants, wealth, and eternal prosperity to them and their heirs forever; for the soil of Louisiana was said to bear two crops a year without cultivation, and the amiable savages were said so to adore the white man that they would not allow these superior beings to labor, and would themselves, voluntarily and for mere love, assume all the burden of that sordid necessity. Endless variations were played upon the themes of gold and silver mines, pearl fisheries, a balmy climate that abolished disease and old age, and a soil that had but to be tickled to give up, almost as one wished, either the smiling harvest or the laughing gold."

Father Charlevoix wrote that these new arrivals were "miserable wretches driven from France for real or supposed crimes." They felt exiled and could scarcely care less about "the progress of a colony of which they are only members in spite of themselves." Bienville was outraged. He wrote to Philippe: "All I have is a band of deserters, smugglers and scoundrels, who are ready not only to abandon you but also...to turn against you."

John Law's vast scheme collapsed in 1720. In four years he had managed to double the size of France's debt. He left scores of Frenchmen bankrupt and homeless. Only Law himself amassed the promised vast fortune with which he had lured the French. He was exiled from France and spent the remaining five years of his life gambling away all that he had acquired from honest folk. He died in Vienna in 1725.

New Orleans finally began to flourish. Bienville reorganized The Company of the West into The Company of the Indies. More importantly, he laid out the streets of his village to a grid pattern – still obvious today and, by the river, he reserved a square which he called the Place d'Armes (now Jackson Square) as a parade ground. He planned a church and rectory, as well as a barracks and a prison. He gave his streets the names of his patrons in France, names like Bourbon, Royal and St. Louis, as well as Conti and Toulouse.

The first census of New Orleans was taken in 1721 and it counted a free, white population of 290 men, 140 women and ninety-six children. In addition, there were 156 indentured white servants, 533 black slaves and fifty Indian slaves. There were also thirty-six cows and nine horses.

Slaves had first been imported by Bienville from the West Indies in 1708. Many were imported during subsequent years. The French certainly did not want to dirty their hands by tilling their own soil. Besides, it was simply too hot and humid. They reasoned that black slaves, especially those from Africa, were used to this kind of heat. Black slaves became essential to white settlers for civilized life in New Orleans.

Compared to the English, Dutch and Spanish, the French had different ideas about colonization. Unlike the English, for example, they had long forbidden religious dissenters (that meant Protestants) to emigrate to Louisiana or Canada. They became concerned about black people too.

Bienville decided to codify the sentiments of his colony, resulting in his famous *Code Noir* in 1721. This banned Jews from the colony and prohibited the Protestants who were brave enough to come at all, such as the nearby Germans, from worshipping. It also prohibited whitemen from marrying Negroes. On the positive side, however, the code also forbade masters from working their slaves on Sunday, and required that they instruct them in the ways of the Lord. It also permitted marriages between slaves and forbade any slave sale that would split up a slave home.

The most persistent problem faced by Bienville was where to find that pool of able-bodied, hard-working settlers who would eventually turn his silt-laden land into an oasis. The men that he had preferred hunting to farming. Unlike the English, who settled their colonies with families, the French had imported mostly men – many of whom came unwillingly. At one point, in 1719, Philippe conscripted 299 women from various prisons, but that proved disastrous.

Jealousies and dissent had always plagued Bienville's tenure as governor. In 1724 he was stripped of his title again, but this time he was recalled to France and forbidden to return to the city he loved.

When he left, his military commander said: "The troops are without discipline, arms or ammunition, most of the time without clothing, and they are frequently obliged to seek their food among the Indian tribes. This is a country which, to the shame of France, be it said, is without religion, without discipline, without order and without police."

The arrival of a band of Ursuline nuns in 1727 helped improve matters partially. Bienville had long hoped to see this order of teaching sisters set up a school, hospital and an orphanage in New Orleans. With their arrival came hopes for a civilized society. The idealism of these young girls is caught in the spirit of a letter sent by Sister Madeleine Hachard de Saint-Stanislas to her father: "Our town is very beautiful, well laid out and evenly built, as well as I can tell. The streets are wide and straight. The main street is a league long. The houses are well built of timber and mortar. Their tops are covered with shingles, which are little planks, sharpened in the form of slates, one must see them to believe it for this roofing has all the appearance and beauty of slate. There is a popular song sung here which says that the city is as beautiful as Paris. Perhaps the song could convince people who have not seen the capital of France, but I have seen it, and the song does not persuade me to the contrary."

Could this be the same town that Father Charlevoix had described only seven years earlier? Sister Hachard went on to say to her father:

"We have a farmyard and a garden which adjoins a great wood of huge trees. From these woods come clouds of mosquitoes, gnats, and another kind of fly that I never met before and whose name or surname I do not know. At this moment several are sailing around me and wish to assassinate me. These wicked animals bite without mercy. We are assailed by them all night, but happily they go back to the woods in the day...We drink beer, and our most ordinary food is rice with a little milk, litle wild beans, meat and fish. In summer we eat little meat...It is a charming country all winter, and in summer there are the fish and oysters, fruits and sweet potatoes, which one cooks in the ashes, like chestnuts." ... "The women are careless of their salvation, but not of their vanity." She wrote "Everyone here has luxuries, all of an equal magnificence. The greater part of them eat hominy but are dressed in velvet or damask, trimmed with ribbons. The women use powder and rouge to hide the wrinkles of their faces, and wear beauty-spots. The devil has a vast empire here, but that only strengthens our hope of destroying it, God willing."

Finally, in 1728, the government tried an entirely new tack in an effort to entice much-desired hard-working settlers. They brought in the "casket girls." These were women of good families and marriageable age who were recruited to go to New Orleans to marry upstanding, eligible men. They arrived with a small wardrobe consisting of two dresses, two petticoats, six headdresses, ribbons, buttons and bows. They got their name from the small suitcase they carried, becoming known as *filles à la cassette*. They continued to arrive on a regular basis for the next thirty years. Attracted by the prospect of good women and prospective wives, more men came to New Orleans. By 1731, it boasted a population of 7,500. Bienville's dreams seemed to be coming true, but without Bienville. He would return one day, but not before another disastrous turn of events had taken its course.

The French had always enjoyed excellent relations with the resident Indians, unlike the English colonists. They attempted to deal with them as equals rather than savages and it had paid off. Nevertheless, in 1729, the French ran into serious trouble with the warrior nation of the Natchez.

It all started when Bienville established Fort Rosalie upstream. A Captain Chepard decided that he wanted a choice piece of land for his own plantation just outside the Fort walls, but the said land was the site of an Indian sacred burial ground and temple. The Natchez requested at least two months to harvest their crops, and then they would consider the grant. Chepard, however, delivered an ultimatum requiring an immediate decision.

The Natchez had been put in a difficult position. Gaining access to the Fort under the guise of a ceremony in honor of Chepard, they attacked. Estimates of those killed range from 300 to 700.

If that had been the end of it, the incident might not hold such a prominent place in history. Instead, the Governor of New Orleans imagined that all the Negroes were in league with the Indians. They were threatened with death unless they proved their innocence by attacking Indians. In addition, Indian nation was pitted against Indian nation; the Natchez against the Tunica and the whites against the entire Natchez and Chickasaw tribes. Eventually, the Natchez were driven from Louisiana and the Chickasaw too. The Choctaw managed, by cunning, to remain on the fringe of the war, avoiding the enmity of whitemen and Indian nation alike. Their reward was to be allowed to remain on their land.

In the midst of all this dissention, The Company of the Indies folded and Louisiana became a crown colony again. Bienville was returned to his old post of governor. He served with distinction in that capacity for another twelve years until he asked to return to France in 1743.

His replacement was a French nobleman whose father was Governor-General of Canada. Pierre Rigaud, Marquis de Vaudreuil, was a typical eighteenth-century aristocrat. He was courtly and refined and his wife was socially ambitious. They patronized the arts as well as founding hospitals, and they entertained on a lavish scale. Balls, fetes and extravagant banquets served on gold plates became the custom in New Orleans.

It was probably during Vaudreuil's tenure that the first official Mardi Gras celebration was held in New Orleans.

Perhaps as many as fifty centuries beforehand, Greek peasants began celebrating the longed-for arrival of spring. They would sacrifice a goat and run naked through the fields pursued by a pagan priest who would lightly whip them with a piece of goatskin as atonement for their sins. The Romans later turned the custom into an orgy. Christianity brought a new development to the celebration. No amount of Christian guilt could persuade people to give up their traditional spring celebration, so the Church adopted this annual spring rite as a feast to precede the Lenten period of atonement and penance. They called it *carnem levare*, Latin for farewell to meat.

Even by the seventeenth century, the event was chiefly an Italian tradition, but it had incorporated an artistic pageantry. Dances and theatre productions were common. In eighteenth-century Venice, the population adopted the practise of masking.

France did not start celebrating the rite of spring until a relatively late date. When it did, the French popularized masked balls and introduced the *boeuf gras*, or giant bull, that has since come to symbolize the Mardi Gras celebration. Louis XV brought a new elegance to the celebration by holding grand masked balls at Versailles. This was the much-loved tradition that Vaudreuil instituted in New Orleans.

Vaudreuil and his wife presided over a grand society in New Orleans for fifteen years until he was promoted to Governor-General of Canada, the post that had been held by his father for so long. New Orleans folk had loved Vaudreuil. His successor would not be so fortunate. Louis Billouart de Kerlerec's colony would be given away during his tenure.

Louis XV had grown tired of subsidizing his colony in the New World with nary a cache of gold to show for it. Furthermore, he was involved in another war, the Seven Years' War, which pitted the combined forces of France and Spain against England – merely following in his grandfather's footsteps perhaps. So, in 1762, Louis gave Louisiana to his cousin Charles III of Spain. However, as with most French intrigues, it was kept secret until after Great Britain won the Seven Years' War. The French and Spanish monarchs now signed a treaty with the English, ceding all territory east of the Mississippi, including Canada and Florida, to Great Britain. Only New Orleans would remain French. As far as the English knew, the rest of Louisiana was French as well. Only the French and Spanish knew that the rest of Louisiana was really Spanish. Spain's control now extended from the Mississippi westward almost to its Californian lands on the Pacific Coast.

The question was what would Spain do with Louisiana? Nothing, apparently. The French governor remained to administer Louisiana. The English had control of the Mississippi, and their ships could be seen passing New Orleans with increasing frequency, but there were no Spaniards lining the banks to watch them pass.

In fact, it was four years before a Spanish governor arrived. When he did, he met a French population that had built up a wellhead of resentment and indignation. After all, they were French citizens! The ultimate insult came when the new governor forbade the sale of the beloved French Bordeaux wine and insisted that the people drink the distasteful Spanish version instead. That was too much.

Eventually, in 1768, the French had had enough. Five hundred rebels marched through the streets of New Orleans shouting *Vive la France*! Stealing through town under the cover of darkness, the Spanish Governor climbed aboard a ship and sailed off into the night. So much for Spanish rule.

Or so thought the French, but no more than nine months later they were to train their eyes on the horizon, hardly believing what they saw. Up the river came twenty-four Spanish galleons with 2,500 men aboard – power credentials the French could understand.

The new Spanish Governor was a man with the unlikely name of General Alexander O'Reilly, and he wasted no time in flying the Spanish flag. O'Reilly was not actually Spanish, he had fled the English as a persecuted Catholic, and had especially endeared himself to King Charles of Spain by saving his life. In return, O'Reilly had been granted increasingly responsible government positions.

He probably did not like New Orleans much because he only stayed for seven months, but in that time he left no doubt that French "Louisiane" was now Spanish Louisiana. He abolished all French laws except the *Code Noir*, took a census that determined there were now 3,190 people in New Orleans (not including the 2,500 Spanish soldiers), and instituted a tax on all places of amusement. He levied a forty-dollar tax on taverns and a twenty-dollar tax on boarding houses and coffee houses. It would be interesting to know what was going on in these wicked places to merit such a stiff tax.

However, he also gave all settlers a plot of land of their own to farm. This, of course, increased loyalty to Spain, not to mention food production, and the time was ripe to welcome some new settlers.

France had settled Acadia (Nova Scotia) in 1605 but, after the Seven Years' War when Great Britain acquired the land, the British demanded loyalty of these French Canadians – a proud and stubborn people. Never would they swear allegiance to Great Britain, they declared. England would not tolerate such rebelliousness. They were all exiled, and they were exiled with total disregard for families. Husbands were split from wives and children from mothers. For years the Acadians wandered in search of their missing family members. Some were never reunited, some returned to France, but others drifted south.

The Acadians, or Cajuns, who finally reached

Louisiana found it to their liking. They were farm folk and the Spanish offered them free land, tools and livestock if they would stay. By 1785 there were approximately 5,000 Acadians living out in the bayou and prairie lands. Today there are almost 500,000. They retain their own language, which they insist is the same pure French their ancestors spoke in 1605, and they retain a pride in their own culture, especially in their music and food.

Cajun food is pungent and spicy, using fresh, local ingredients from the sea and swamps: crab, oysters, shrimp, crawfish; and from the land: frogs, turtles, ducks, yams, pecans, beans and okra.

Cajun music has a character all its own. Its most popular themes are family, love, friendship and fun. It is a contagious, happy music just made for foot-stomping and hand-clapping. When the music is performed in the traditional style, it is played on two fiddles, an accordion and a triangle – but modern renditions sometimes use drums, guitars, mandolins and spoons, as well as the fiddles.

Acadian country out on Bayou Teche is known as Evangeline country after a young woman called Emmeline Labiche. The story goes that a lovely, black-haired girl by the name of Emmeline Labiche lived in Acadia during the eighteenth century. She was an orphan. At sixteen years of age she fell in love with Louis Arceneaux and they planned to wed. The day before the wedding the British forced the Acadians into exile. Emmeline and Louis were separated. No matter where she was sent, Emmeline looked only for the face of Louis. She was sent first one place and then another. She searched and searched. She asked wherever she went for news about her lover, but to no avail.

She eventually arrived in the bayou country just outside New Orleans. Still she had not found Louis. Until one day, sitting under a tree, she came upon him. Her heart stopped. She ran up to him, threw her arms around him, only to have him say that he had despaired of finding her again and had eventually pledged himself to another. Emmeline was distraught. She lost her mind, spending her days wandering aimlessly through fields of wildflowers, and dying soon after the encounter.

Nathaniel Hawthorne heard the tale some time in the 1840s and related it to his friend Henry Wadsworth Longfellow. It spurred the renowned poet to learn all he could about the Acadian exodus and the bayou country. His poem on the subject does not follow the original tale exactly, but the Cajuns have adopted it as their own.

Longfellow's epic poem immortalizes the Acadian migration with simplicity and sympathy. It is called simply *Evangeline*:

"This is the forest primeval; but where are the hearts that beneath it

Leaped like the roe when he hears in the woodland the voice of the huntsman?

Where is the thatch-roofed village, the home of Acadian farmers,

Men whose lives glided on like rivers that water the woodlands,

Darkened by shadows of earth, but reflecting an image of heaven?

Waste are those pleasant farms, and the farmers for ever departed

Scattered like dust and leaves, when the mighty blasts of October

Seize them, and whirl them aloft, and sprinkle them far o'er the ocean;

Naught but tradition remains of the beautiful village of Grand- Pre'

Ye who believe in affection that hopes, and endures, and is patient,

Ye who believe in the beauty and strength of woman's devotion,

List to the mournful tradition still sung by the pines of the forest;

List to a Tale of Love in Acadie, home of the happy …

Still stand the forest primeval; but under the shade of its branches

Dwells another race, with other customs and language. Only along the shore of the mournful and misty Atlantic Linger a few Acadian peasants, whose fathers from exile Wandered back to their native land to die in its bosom ..." Emmeline Labiche is buried in the churchyard of St. Martin de Tours Church in the village of St. Martinville. Delores Del Rio, the actress who played the title role in the movie based on Emmeline's life, posed for the statue of "Evangeline" atop Emmeline's tomb. The tomb is still a popular tourist attraction.

The Revolutionary War to the north of New Orleans did not really affect the town much. French sympathies certainly lay with the stubborn Americans, but New Orleans had troubles enough of its own without poking its nose into the business of others. Few men even bothered to enlist, regardless of the example set by General Lafayette.

Life in New Orleans improved under the Spanish. One account of the city in 1776 was recorded by Don Francisco de Bouligny: "The inhabitants of this country may be divided into three classes; planters, merchants and day-laborers... The greater number of planters who live in the vicinity of New Orleans are the most refined people in this country... The second class – the merchants – are occupied only in buying and selling and in making occasional journeys to distant posts, eager to be able to earn enough to become planters... The third class work two or three days in the week, and spend the remainder of their time in the taverns. The houses are convenient, according to the climate; all have a very wide gallery or covered balcony which surrounds them for protection against the intense heat of the summer, and there are fireplaces in all the rooms for the winter, which sometimes is severe. The houses are thirty feet from the bank of the river, because they are pleasanter thus, and it is easier to embark and debark, as everything is conducted by water. The houses are of wood, brick and mortar, and the kitchen is about twenty paces to the rear of the house. There is a garden or orchard, especially in the country."

Indeed life in New Orleans had improved dramatically, but the town was not destined to remain the town it had become. Two disastrous fires were responsible for totally transforming the city.

The first occurred on Good Friday, 1788, when a lighted candle on a home altar ignited draperies. There was a strong wind and soon most of the town was ablaze. Since it was Good Friday, the priests refused to allow the church bells to be rung, so no alarm was sounded. New Orleans had a population in 1788 of 5,338 residents. In all, 856 houses were destroyed, for a total loss of $2,595,561.00. By some miracle, the Ursaline Convent, set back off the street behind a walled garden, was spared. It is one of the oldest buildings in New Orleans today.

No sooner had they started rebuilding than a second fire swept the town in 1794. This time it destroyed 212 buildings. Although both fires were tragic, they proved to be blessings in disguise. It was recorded that: "What lay in the ashes was, at best, but an irregular, ill-built French town, while what arose from them was a stately Spanish city, proportioned with grace and built with solidity."

The Spanish houses that grew from the ashes of the French Quarter were made of brick and stucco, with arches of heavy masonry and Spanish tile roofs. There were long, shadowy corridors that entered into patios with splashing fountains, and overhanging balconies ornamented with hand-crafted, filigreed, wrought-iron work. Even the public buildings, including the St. Louis Cathedral and the Cabildo were rebuilt to be far superior to their smaller predecessors.

The Spanish built a small, intimate town. Citizens painted their houses in pastel greens, blues and pinks. Sidewalks were paved with brick or flagstone and shells were added to make them more stable.

Major Stoddard visited New Orleans in 1812 and left this description of the rebuilt houses: "Among them is an elegant brick house covered with tile. Several of them were two stories high and two in the same quarter three stories high. One of them cost $80,000 and the rest from $15 to 20,000. They are all plastered on the outside with white or colored mortar..."

It was during Spanish stewardship too that a potential disaster of greater magnitude even than the fires was diverted. In 1788 a Spanish monk, Antonio de Sedella, arrived from Spain. His mission had been kept a deep secret but he announced on his arrival that he had been appointed Commissary for the Inquisition and was instructed to establish a tribunal in New Orleans.

Fortunately for New Orleans, Governor Miro immediately had Sedella arrested and shipped back to Spain. Yet, fifty years later, historians uncovered a chilling truth when the old jail located next to the church was destroyed. They wrote: "...Strange things came to light. There were found secret rooms, iron instruments of torture, and other indications that a private court had held meetings there. In addition to this, old newspaper files tell of the discovery of an underground passage which led from the rear of the Cathedral, or from even beyond that point in the direction of the Capuchin Monastery – a passage which ended somewhere under the Calaboose."

Nonetheless, the Spanish were good administrators. It was recorded that Louisiana enjoyed greater growth and prosperity during the last ten or fifteen years of Spanish rule than in all of its previous history. The Port of New Orleans was greatly expanded. In 1799, 256 ocean liners called at the port. Spain changed the primary agricultural products from indigo and tobacco to cotton and sugar cane.

If you have ever wondered where the term "two bits" came from it arose because Spanish silver coins were so scarce that they sometimes had to be cut in half. Two bits of silver could be spent twice as fast as one. Although Spanish rule had been good for New Orleans, in 1800 Spain ceded Louisiana back to France. As usual, it was almost three years before the French took possession. In fact, official possession never did take place. In 1803 the people of Louisiana, waiting for the French army to arrive, saw a single French ship sail into the harbor. It carried notification that Louisiana had been sold to the United States.

There had been no viable government in New Orleans for over three years. Gambling and prostitution were flourishing. However, it did not take the United States as long to claim their land as it had the French or Spanish. They arrived on December 20, 1803, and raised the "Stars and Stripes."

What had led to the sale of Louisiana to the United States? Napoleon's hopes to conquer Haiti could not be realized and were finally abandoned in 1791. President Thomas Jefferson, though he loved France, recognized that the French had the power to close the Port of New Orleans whenever they wanted, and this was decidedly not good for the United States. He wrote: "There is on this globe a single spot, the possessor of which is the natural and habitual enemy of the United States. It is New Orleans ... through which the produce of three-eighths of our territory must pass to market."

Robert Livingstone, the minister to France, had been negotiating with the French for three years, but with no success. Only Napoleon could make such a decision, but he was off campaigning. On the other hand, Napoleon did not want the British to have Louisiana. Finally, in 1803, he made his decision. Not only would he sell New Orleans to the Americans, but he would sell them all of the Louisiana territory for fifteen million dollars – four cents an acre. It amounted to 825,000 square miles, fully one third of a subcontinent. It was so large that all or a part of thirteen of our present states were carved from it. It was one of the best real estate deals in history except, perhaps, for the purchase of Manhattan Island from the Indians for twenty-four dollars.

Napoleon knew full well what he was doing. He said: "I know all the value of Louisiana and I have wished to repair the error of the French negotiator who abandoned it in 1763. A few lines of a treaty have given it back to me and hardly have I recovered it when I must expect to lose it. But if I lose it, it will be dearer one day to those who compel me to abandon it than to those to whom I wish to deliver it. The English have successively taken away from France Canada, Cape Breton, Newfoundland, Acadia, the richest parts of Asia. They shall not have the Mississippi which they covet ... The conquest of Louisiana would be easy if they merely took the trouble to land there. I have not a moment to lose if I wish to place it out of their reach."

Oddly enough, the greatest disputes under the new administration did not take place in the business houses or the courts, but at the many balls that New Orleans folks attended nightly. The new Americans would demand that the orchestra play an English quadrille, while the French insisted on the French version. Tempers would flare and satisfaction was likely as not found at the Dueling Oaks. Dueling had become so common that scarcely a man in public life had not fought one. It seemed to be one of the requirements of public office.

Dueling was probably more common in New Orleans than anywhere else in the United States. A journalist wrote: "The least breach of etiquette, the least suspicion cast of unfair dealings, an aspersion against the moon, the night, the temperature ... almost anything can provoke a challenge."

The *Code Duello* outlined the rules in grim detail. It defined the difference between a slight, an insult and an offense, and it prescribed the methods of redress for each. Dueling was embraced by the Americans in New Orleans with cold-blooded regularity. One difference existed, however. The Creoles declared that satisfaction had been won at the first show of blood. The Americans were in it to the death.

If life in town was not always gentile, life on the river most certainly was not. The steamboat had not yet been invented, so a boat called the keelboat was in general use. It was usually fifty to seventy feet long, eighteen feet wide and pointed at the bow and stern and it was the only means of carrying cargo on the river.

These boats were crewed by rough, tough men called Kaintocks. When they were relaxing in New Orleans they were wild and undisciplined. They loved a good fight, and a good fight would invariably include biting, gouging, kicking, stomping, stabbing, clubbing and anything else equally unthinkable.

Starting a fight was always the most fun. They would face each other, leap into the air, crack their heels together and shout fierce war cries, each more ferocious than the next.

When Abe Lincoln was a boy he thought it would be great fun to have an adventure on one of these keelboats. He signed on at eight dollars a month for a three-month trip to "Orleans." A scar over his right eye for the rest of his life attested to the rough and tumble life of the Kaintocks. One night while he was sleeping, he was rousted out by a gang of thieves, who set upon him. It must not have been too bad though, because he signed on for one more keelboat trip after that.

Whenever there are stories of wild, uncontrolled men, their women are not far behind, often even more ferocious than their menfolk. Annie Christmas was no exception. She tipped the scales at over two hundred and fifty pounds, stood six feet eight inches tall and sported a cute little mustache. Strength she had in abundance and she was a fearless fighter. To put fear into her opponents, it is said that she wore a necklace containing a bead for every nose or ear she had chewed off. It is rumored that it was thirty feet long when she died.

If you have ever wondered what a "Dixie" was or where the name came from we can thank the Kaintocks for the term. The American monetary system was in a shambles when the United States purchased Louisiana. To ease the situation, a New Orleans bank started issuing ten-dollar notes – one side in English and the other in French. The word for ten in French is *dix*, and that is simply what the river men started calling these strange notes. More than one *dix* were called "dixies." Before long, "Dixie" became a place name – denoting New Orleans at first, and then becoming the name for all of the South.

The transition in New Orleans from French/Spanish lifestyle to American was difficult in many ways. For example, the old guard – the aristocratic French and Spanish families – shunned Americans socially unless a meeting could not be avoided. To make the distinction clear, they started referring to themselves as "Creoles" – the French and Spanish certainly did not want anyone to think they were American. They needed a way to tell the world that they were the "old blood," in many cases descended from French and Spanish nobility. Consequently, the term Creole has come to mean native-born, of French or Spanish background and often aristocratic. Creole cooking, Creole language and Creole music still refer to the "old ways."

William C.C. Claiborne was named Governor of the new American possessions. On his arrival, he wrote to President Jefferson that he found the people generally honest, "but they are uninformed, indolent, luxurious – in a word, ill-fitted to be useful citizens of a Republic. Under the Spanish, education was discouraged and little respectability attached to science. Wealth alone gave respect and influence ... hence ignorance and wealth generally pervade this part of Louisiana." Nevertheless, Claiborne served as Governor for thirteen years and was responsible for Louisiana's admission to the Union in 1812 as the eighteenth state.

Perhaps Claiborne's greatest challenge was the swashbuckling privateer, Jean Lafitte. One pictures a dashing rogue sporting plumed, wide-brimmed hats and dapper clothes. Errol Flynn's characters in later movies must have been patterned after Lafitte. Lafitte was a blacksmith by day and a buccaneer by night. He had arrived in 1806 and set up his blacksmith shop in New Orleans. His plundering took place from the heart of Barataria Bay. It is reputed that he had as many as 1,000 men in his employ at one time. His little smuggler's ships would scuttle out to prey on Spanish ships and then slip back into Barataria Bay. He set up sales outlets all along the Gulf Coast. Officials were cut in on the action and there was profit for all.

Legends of Lafitte the Pirate abound. He set up his headquarters on Grand Terre, a screened piece of land hidden among the swamps and bayous of Barataria Bay, some sixty miles south of New Orleans. He and his band gradually developed a network of supplies and contraband merchandise of every description, which they sold to the merchants of New Orleans at prices so low importers could not compete. He has been called a pirate, a murderer and a villain. He has also been called a staunch patriot, a much misunderstood man, a gentleman smuggler and so on.

Jean had a brother, Pierre, who helped in his enterprise. They were quite prosperous and entertained lavishly in their mansion at Bourbon and St. Philip Streets in New Orleans' French Quarter. Prior to 1808, Lafitte had directed the activities on Barataria Bay in a gentlemanly manner from his home but, on January 1, 1808, a law was passed prohibiting the importation of slaves. Suddenly there was a much larger black market to tend to – and a much more lucrative one. Negroes had become an important article of merchandise and their price was rising rapidly.

It was at this point that Jean Lafitte moved to Barataria Bay. He was a very gifted organizer and pulled all the warring factions together, organizing a village on Grand Terre of thatched cottages for the pirates and their women, and building himself a grand brick mansion. His home was supplied with the finest furniture, rugs, china, glassware and silver – all plundered from unsuspecting merchant ships. In it he entertained plantation owners who came to buy his slaves and his old friends from New Orleans in luxurious style.

About this time, the War of 1812 began. For reasons known only to himself – possibly from pure patriotism – Lafitte became involved. In 1814, the Commander of the British Navy came to Lafitte, offering him $30,000 if he would pledge his men, ships and ammunition to the British for a planned invasion of New Orleans. Lafitte instead notified Governor Claiborne of the intended invasion and offered his men in service to the United States. At first turning down the offer, General Andrew "Old Hickory" Jackson finally accepted when he learned of the dismal defenses available in New Orleans. He needed the help of the Lafitte brothers and their men.

The Battle of New Orleans has gone down in history as a most unusual battle. In the first place, the peace treaty had been signed two weeks beforehand, but word of it did not reach Louisiana in time. That is why this has been called "the Battle that Missed the War." Nevertheless, had the British won, the aforesaid peace treaty might have amounted to nothing because it was not actually ratified until one month after the Battle of New Orleans.

General Jackson was Commander of the United States forces in the South and was having a devil of a time. He faced General Sir Edward Packenham, who brought with him 10,000 crack English soldiers. They were the most experienced military force in Europe. They were frequently heard to brag they had "licked Napoleon once a week during the Peninsula Campaign." These were the same troops who had five months earlier marched into Washington unimpeded and burned the White House.

Jackson had command of a motley crew, an army quickly organized from the slaves, dandies, plantation owners, Indians, backwoodsmen and farmers from Tennessee and Kentucky, and the pirates. There were 2,000 at most and very few had fought in a battle before. Furthermore, he had no more than 700 rifles. Jackson believed his best defense was to dig ramparts in a solid line from the river to the swamp out on the Chalmette plain. His men could use that as a barricade.

General Packenham was no fool. He launched a surprise attack at night and captured a plantation at the edge of the ramparts. Jackson, never known for his cool, roared: "By the Eternal, they shall not sleep on our soil" – and the battle was on. Not waiting for daylight, he blackened the faces of a small contingent of his soldiers and attacked with tomahawks, knives and clubs, whooping and yelling all the time. That did the trick. Not knowing how many more heathens might be lurking in the darkness, the British fled. The time lapsing before the British attacked again gave the Americans time to finish the ramparts.

Finally, in early January, 1815, Packenham launched a full attack. Under cover of fog, the well-formed line of British soldiers marched to drum cadence across the plain toward the American line. Merely 200 yards from the line, the fog lifted to reveal a solid line of soldiers, fully armed, just waiting for the order to fire. It must have been an awful moment for the British. Jackson gave the command and the report of 500 long rifles shattered the still air. In fifteen minutes the British could take no more. They broke and ran in total disarray.

Packenham reformed his troops and personally led them into that spitting agony again, only to be shot from his horse and killed. Again and again, the scene was repeated. The crack soldiers of the Royal Highland Regiment in full regalia were mowed down, their bagpipes still wheezing. The British lost over 2,000 men, the Americans only seven.

Regardless of past activities, Lafitte exonerated himself and his men in the Battle of New Orleans. They fought well and they were loyal. General Jackson himself said: "Captains Dominique and Béluche, lately commanding privateers at Barataria, with part of their former crews and many brave citizens of New Orleans, were stationed at Batteries Three and Four. The General cannot avoid giving his warm approbation of the manner in which these gentlemen have uniformly conducted themselves while under his command, and of the gallantry with which they redeemed the pledge they gave at the opening of the campaign to defend the country. The brothers Lafitte have exhibited the same courage and fidelity, and the General promises that the government shall be duly apprised of their conduct."

What now for a famous pirate? At first Lafitte thought about becoming a legitimate businessman in New Orleans, but gave up that idea when he perceived that the local folk would never accept him into their society, no matter how genteel he became. Therefore, he set out with about one hundred of his men, having been given a pardon from the United States for all past crimes. He roamed the seas looking for the right spot, and finally settled on an island off the coast of Texas. He called it "Galvez-town" – later to be changed to Galveston. He was never again to establish a comparable pirate community and his fortunes dwindled. He finally died of a fever in 1826. His legacy is the folk-hero legends about him and the founding of Galveston. International celebrity status continues to mark the name of Jean Lafitte. After the Battle of New Orleans, Lord Byron wrote *The Corsair* with buccaneer Lafitte in mind. It ends: "He left a corsair's name to other times / Linked with one virtue, and a thousand crimes!"

Lafitte's most trusted captains, Dominique You, Réné Béluche and Cut-Nose Chighizola had better luck. Both You and Béluche returned later to New Orleans and became successful businessmen. Cut Nose asked General Jackson to help, and obtained a commission as Commodore of the Navy of Venezuela.

"Here comes a steamboat!" Children dashed to the levee to watch. Bearded gentlemen with gold-tipped canes and ladies in bonnets and hooped skirts all crowded the banks to see. In 1807 Robert Fulton successfully navigated a steamboat up the Hudson River from New York to Albany. In 1812, it was time to try the mighty Mississippi. He built the

The Quadroon Balls were splendidly decorated – even more so than the white balls. Attendance was limited to mulatto girls who were fashionably gowned in the latest styles, often in dresses from New York or Paris. Admission was restricted to white men of means. The admission price was very high. There was never any rowdiness. The whole affair was quite proper and highly stylized.

The finest bands in New Orleans would play. The gentlemen would dance with one and then another elegant woman. If he was especially taken with a particularly charming woman, he would declare his affection and make her an offer. The mother was always in attendance and daughter would immediately refer the whole matter to her. Mother would inquire into the financial terms and, if satisfied, would require security that the gentleman would support her daughter and make her a settlement if he should ever leave. These "arrangements" usually ended when the man married. Then the girl would either marry a mulatto man or, sometimes, open a business of her own.

Harriet Martineau described these events in 1837: "The girls are highly educated and are, probably, as beautiful and accomplished a set of women as can be found. Every young man early selects one, and establishes her in one of those pretty and peculiar houses, whole rows of which may be seen in the Ramparts. The connection now and then lasts for life; usually for several years. In the latter case, when the time comes for the gentleman to take a white wife, the dreadful news reaches his quadroon partner either by letter entitling her to call the house and furniture her own, or by the newspaper which announces the marriage."

Quadroon Balls became quite a tourist attraction too. The Duke of Saxe-Weimar was entranced by these exotic beauties: "resembling the higher orders of women among the high-class Hindoos; lovely countenances, full, dark, liquid eyes; lips of coral; teeth of pearl; sylph-like figures; their beautifully rounded limbs, exquisite gait and ease of manner might furnish models for a Venus or Hebe."

Creole women, however, were not at all happy about all this fuss. The quadroons were completely ostracized by Creole ladies, who usually chose to pretend they did not exist. When they had to acknowledge their presence, it was either by putting them in their place or, perhaps, as the butt of their humor. Creole women are known to have attended masked Quadroon Balls – probably to see if they could catch their husbands in an infidelity. After all, lovely quadroons posed a direct threat to the security of Creole women. To placate them somewhat, the law gave a white woman the right to have a quadroon flogged, almost on whim.

Creole women were always prim and proper on the exterior. They were raised under strictured conditions, never being allowed to be in the company of a man without a chaperone until their wedding night. Weddings, of course, were not usually affairs of the heart, but arranged between parents in the drawing room.

By 1850 the popularity of the Quadroon Balls had declined and, by the Civil War, they had died out altogether. New Orleans was now a metropolitan city of 125,000 people and had outgrown this type of exotic display. By 1879, the New Orleans Times said that since 1864, quadroons had "disappeared from public gaze and, if they exist at all, those of the new generation are utterly shut out from the outside world." Some did travel north, where they were often able to pass as whites. Others married black men.

John McDonough was a male quadroon, but he was certainly an exception to the general rule. McDonough was a man of means. He owned a large plantation, and he sometimes had as many as 200 slaves of his own. But that was where his similarity to the wealthy whites stopped. He was considered a radical. He treated his slaves with humanity, educated them, taught them a craft and then freed them. He said: "They were my men of business. They enjoyed my confidence, collected my rents, leased my houses, took care of my property and effects of every kind. Those I retained were men of honesty and integrity, and I trained them in a trade for a new life."

In his day, McDonough was ridiculed. He bore the brunt of cartoonists' jokes. But when he died in 1850, he was the richest man and the largest landowner in Louisiana. He left a fortune of three million dollars – and all to the children of New Orleans. He wanted poor children to have the advantage of education currently unavailable to them. Within the next ninety years over thirty-five schools were built in his name. His maxims: "Time is Gold, Throw not a Minute Away," "Never Spend but to Produce," "Remember Always, Labor Is One of the Conditions of Our Existence," stand as a memorial to him on his tombstone.

Negroes of pure black blood were not as fortunate as the quadroons. Few whites felt a responsibility for them, but they did recognize that they needed a bit of entertainment at times. So there was not too much concern when the Negroes got together for a little gospel singing on a Sunday afternoon. Sometimes it continued well into the night. The preferred spot for their singing meetings was a large open space at Rampart and Orleans Streets in the French Quarter. It was known as Congo Square. It became more and more popular.

When the gospel singing progressed to dancing, white folks got more worried. It was acceptable for the black folk to have fun, but not too much fun. They finally passed a law in 1817 that decreed: "The assembles of slaves for the purpose of dancing or other merriment, shall take place only on Sundays, and solely in such open or public places as shall be appointed by the Mayor." Congo Square was the place and the law was soon amended to require that the merriment be discontinued at sundown. Congo Square reached the height of popularity in 1845.

Dancers, finely arrayed in brightly colored shirts and dresses, the women with hair in red, blue and green bandanas, would arrive at midday. Chattering white people and other onlookers would line the edges of the Square in anticipation. Just off to the side would be the hawkers of refreshments – selling lemonade, ginger beer, pies and ginger cakes.

At a signal from the police – for the police were always present – a drummer would begin to beat on the head of a cask with two beef bones. This instrument was called a bamboula. The dancers moved to the center of the Square and danced the dances of Africa – the men leaping into the air and strutting and the women gently swaying back and forth to the beat of the drum. Congo Square became another one of those exotic tourist attractions that New Orleans was so famous for.

This period of the first half of the nineteenth century was known as the "Glamour Period." It was during this time that Mardi Gras was revived in earnest. The Spanish had banned public masking because of the crimes they were fearful it might foster, but now it was revived in all its frivolity. However, it was not the French who revived it, it was the American who brought to it unrestrained merrymaking.

The first parade was really a ragtag affair that was merely the continuation of New Year's Eve revelry. High in spirits (in more ways than one), a group of men spilled out of a tavern. They wound in and out of small streets and stopped to serenade friends and the merely curious. At one point along the way the employees of a local hardware store equipped them with rakes to carry. At another, they ran into the mayor, who invited them in for breakfast. The year was 1830. They decided this was so much fun that they would make it an annual event.

The first carnival float appeared in 1838 as a "giant fighting cock that waved and nodded its head, while drawn through the streets by a team of horses." According to the newspaper account, it was "A beautiful joyous cavalcade ... the whole town doubled with laughter."

Sir Charles Lyell described a parade he witnessed in 1846: "There was a great procession parading the streets, almost everyone dressed in the most grotesque attire, troops of them on horseback, some in open carriages, with bands of music, and in a variety of costumes – some as Indians, with feathers in their heads, and one, a jolly, fat man, as Mardi Gras himself. All wore masks, and here and there in the crowd, or stationed in a balcony above, we saw persons armed with bags of flour, which they showered down copiously on any one who seemed particularly fond of his attire."

The only oddity about these parades was that they took place on New Year's Day and everyone knows that Mardi Gras takes place the day before Lent. The French celebrated Mardi Gras already in a quiet, restrained way – with a masked ball perhaps - but these were certainly not open to the Americans.

It became clear how to correct that. Each year a larger and larger group met to discuss the following year's New Year's Day parade. In 1857 they met as usual, this time on February 8th. They decided to make some major changes. They formed a new society calling themselves "The Mistick Krewe of Comus." What on earth, the townsfolk asked, was that all about? It seems that Ben Jonson in *Pleasure Reconciled to Virtue* described a certain Comus, the god of good cheer, who rode "in triumph crowned with flowers and attended by a rabble chorus who sing the song of the Bouncing Belly." That suited the revelers' image just fine.

With all this wild inspiration, no one wanted to wait for next New Year's Day to bring on the band. Why not hold the parade on Mardi Gras? All agreed it was a splendid idea. All except the French. They did not like the idea of Americans encroaching on their party day at all.

The big day arrived and everyone was in for a great treat. The new Comus rode in triumph, crowned with flowers, with two floats in his parade. On one rode the God of Revelry and, on the other, Satan, which was only traditional. Had the first Rites of Spring celebrations not combined revelry with devilry? They were followed by maskers and a thumping, blaring band. The most startling and exciting new novelty, though, was that the parade took place at night. The parade was illuminated by torches that bathed the old streets and houses in a soft, golden glow. It was fun, but it was enchanting too. New Orleans loved it and, moreover, so did the

French.

La Belle Epoche, much as it may appear to us to be, was not merely a time for fancy dress and amusements. It was a time for building too. The French had long laid claim to the French Quarter. When the Americans arrived, they were made to feel that their presence was most unwelcome in this genteel French enclave.

Canal Street was the dividing line between the American segment of New Orleans and the French district. It was called the "neutral zone." Americans settled southwest of Canal Street in the Faubourg Lafayette in what would become known as the Garden District. In 1833 Faubourg Lafayette was granted the status of a town.

Land was plentiful in the Garden District and many wealthy Americans purchased two or three lots. They erected grand, palatial homes with either an elaborately landscaped side garden or spacial lawns and gardens surrounding the entire house. They built their homes in a wild mélange of styles, ranging from Italian Villa, Italianate, Greek Revival and Queen Anne. Their gardens were surrounded by lovely, wrought-iron fences, of elaborate and original design.

These grand homes regularly contained as many as thirty rooms – all of enormous proportions, with ceilings fourteen feet high on the lower floors. They had marble and onyx fireplaces, carved mahogany stairs and plaster moldings, as well as gold-leaf chandeliers and pier glass mirrors.

New Orleans architects understood that high ceilings, floor-to-ceiling windows and transoms over doors allowed better air circulation and coolness. Yet, try as these architects might to design their homes in the classic manner of Europe, they could not resist a few of the traditional Spanish touches that abound in the French Quarter. That is why we can still see the ornamental railings and wide porches and that is partly what makes the district so charming.

By 1860 the Garden District had become the premier residential section of New Orleans – the Americans had accomplished their purpose. However, by 1865, with the Civil War in progress, they virtually discontinued their building project. Houses that were built after the war were smaller and leaner. The era of the grand house was gone. Fortunately, the entire district is now on the *National Register of Historic Places.*

In the 1850s, right next to the Garden District, another district was growing by leaps and bounds. Its residents came by the boatload with merely the clothing on their backs. For the Irish, anything was better than starving in the potato famine in Ireland.

This area would become known as the Irish Channel.

They were a clannish, audacious lot who did not take kindly to strangers. Anyone venturing into the Irish Channel was likely to be greeted with a shower of bricks. The term "Irish Channel" probably came about because whenever it rained in New Orleans, which was and is often, water would pour down the hills from the rich, elevated Garden District into the low-lying, mud-filled channel where the Irish had built their homes.

Although the Irish were hard-working and prospered, they were considered immoral, uncouth ruffians by the rest of the city. As a matter of fact, it was the Irish Channel that gangs of toughs like Rat Tooth Flynn and the Crowbar Gang frequented. It was a lusty, bawdy sort of place, with tough taverns that were host to many drunken brawls and fights. The "Bucket of Blood" and the "Bull's Head" were among the most popular.

The Irish were not slaves, but the wages they earned put them in the same financial category. For the Irish and blackmen it was a hard and often cruel life.

It had been illegal to import slaves since 1807 but they continued to pour in nevertheless. Page after page of classified advertisements appeared in the newspapers. An octoroon girl often brought as much as $7,000, while a field hand would bring $1,500. By 1850 the old *Code Noir* had been abandoned and New Orleans treated its slaves the same way as they were treated in other Southern states. They were sold as any other piece of property. They could not marry, nor testify in court. They could not defend themselves against a white person and it was a crime to teach them to read and write.

Slave owners began to think of slavery as divinely sanctioned and eventually could not conceive of any other way for the two races to live. Moreover, the economy of the South was entirely dependent on slavery.

In Louisiana especially, the sugar and cotton industries depended exclusively on slave labor. It was said: "By one of the great ironies of history, the American democracy took control of this imperial colony (Louisiana) at the moment when the cotton gin was converting America into the greatest slave power in the world. The gin had changed cotton from being a fiber more expensive than silk into the cheapest fiber on earth; and the impact of this change, rich land, mechanical ginning, and Negro slavery, combined to produce very rapidly a powerful new ruling class, the most arrogant and insular *nouveaux riches* in American experience."

By 1850, slavery was the most heated debate issue

in Washington and in all the state houses. It was one of those issues that had no gray middle ground. One was either for or against slavery, but either way one cared passionately. When Abraham Lincoln was elected president in 1860, Louisiana rejected him overwhelmingly. South Carolina seceded from the Union, quickly followed by Mississippi, Alabama and Florida. Louisiana followed one month later.

The South was proud of itself. It had ideals that it defended and stood by. They had heard that there might be a war but they hoped simply to establish a new country and avoid hostilities. However, if war should come, they were prepared to fight.

General Pierre Gustave Toutant Beauregard, a refined Creole gentleman who had been raised on a lovely plantation in St. Bernard, cautioned the military leaders to be sure of the defense of New Orleans from the water, but no one paid much attention. Beauregard then left for Charleston.

It was this same Beauregard who fired the first shot at Fort Sumter in Charleston, beginning the Civil War. He engineered a brilliant defense of the harbor of Charleston and later went on to defend Richmond in 1864. He was also to try in vain to halt General Sherman's march to the sea.

New Orleans did not see any of the war until April of 1862. When she did, however, it was with decisiveness. The Union sea attack was commanded by General David Farragut. He was backed up by land forces under the command of General Benjamin Butler. Farragut rained lead on Fort Jackson and Fort St. Philip for several days.

The Confederate fleet of seven vessels was simply no match for the Union Navy. Weak and untrained, they offered no resistance. All but one ship sank. Finally, Farragut sailed past the forts and landed in New Orleans.

The land forces of General Butler followed closely behind and together they took the city in seven days. Fifteen thousand bales of cotton were burned on the levee, merchant ships were torched, warehouses were seized and looted. For the residents of New Orleans, though, that was only the beginning.

General Butler took control of the city and became its leader during the occupation. No man in the history of New Orleans has ever been so hated and reviled. He was arrogant, obstinate and stubborn. He was also determined to make the Southerners pay for what he saw as their disloyalty.

He brought 18,000 troops with him and ruled with an iron fist. In his words: "New Orleans is a conquered city – conquered by the forces of the United States and lies subject to the will of the conqueror." Unsurprisingly, he became known as

"Beast" Butler. He closed down most of the city newspapers, freely confiscated heirloom silverware because the war effort needed metal, and ordered all the church bells to be melted down and used for Yankee cannon balls. It was just too much. An historian described him: "In war as in peace, Butler was a P.T. Barnum character. Gross in body, he was unscrupulously clever in mind … and incorrigibly political in purpose."

The ladies of New Orleans hated him passionately. They loved to taunt him by wearing Confederate colors to decorate their hats or dresses, whistling Southern songs as they passed him and refusing to stay in the same room as a Yankee soldier. He found their conduct most impolite. As a result, he promulgated the most hated law of all. Officially it was known as General Order Number Twenty-Eight, but everyone called it the "Woman Order." It decreed that any woman engaged in such practices would be treated as a common prostitute, and could be arrested, held overnight in jail and fined five dollars. Small wonder they all hated him so much.

Finally, he issued an order requiring that all foreigners in New Orleans swear allegiance to the United States. This violated all rules of international diplomacy and the outrage was overwhelming. President Lincoln immediately countermanded the order and recalled Butler to New York in late 1862.

Butler's farewell speech to New Orleans is one more example of his egoism: "I do not feel I have erred in too much harshness … I might have smoked you to death in caverns, as were the Covenanters of Scotland by a royal British general, or roasted you like the people of Algiers were roasted by the French; your wives and daughters might have been given over to the ravisher as were the dames of Spain in the Peninsular War, and your property turned over to indiscriminate plunder like that of the Chinese when the English captured their capital; you might have been blown from the mouths of cannons as were the sepoys of Delhi … and kept within the rules of civilized war as practiced by the most polished and hypocritical capitals of Europe. But I have not so conducted!"

1864 was a decisive year. Sherman had captured Atlanta and left it burning as he made his march to the sea. He arrived in Savannah in December, 1864. Sherman sent a triumphant telegram to the newly re-elected President Lincoln, saying he was presenting Savannah to him as a Christmas present. He started his march north to join Grant. He met little resistance along his entire route, even though he destroyed all Southern property in his path. The psychological effects were devastating. With no army to protect them, Southerners could only stand by and watch the parade of soldiers pass them by.

Finally, in April 1865, General Lee surrendered to Grant at Appomattox and General Johnston surrendered to Sherman at Durham. The war was over. Among the officers, a great deal of mutual respect had built up. Grant wrote the terms of the surrender; they were simple and generous. The officers and men were to sign a pledge that they would fight no more and then they could go home. Officers were allowed to retain their sidearms and all who owned their horses were free to take them home with them.

The formal surrender was a ceremony marked by this same respect, as well as sorrow and compassion. Grant designated General Joshua Chamberlain to receive the surrender. As the slow, forlorn gray column passed Chamberlain's line, his men shifted from "order arms" to "marching salute," the highest honor fighting men could give to other fighting men. General Gordon was at the head of the Confederate line, head bowed and in obvious agony. Nevertheless, at this signal, he dropped the point of his sword, wheeled himself and his magnificent horse into upright position and ordered his men to return the salute. Chamberlain later recorded: "On our part not a sound of trumpet more, nor roll of drum; not a cheer, nor word nor whisper of vainglorying, nor mention of man standing again at the order, but an awed stillness rather, and breath-holding, as if it were the passing of the dead!"

Perhaps, had Abraham Lincoln lived, Reconstruction might have been easier. He proposed that Southern states be readmitted to the Union as soon as ten percent of the voting population of 1860 pledged loyalty to the Union. It was his idea that all Southerners who swore allegiance should be pardoned. It is not generally known that Lincoln was not in favor of extending the franchise to the freed Negroes, at least not immediately. Louis Agassiz of Harvard supported Lincoln in this. He wrote: "I cannot, therefore, think it just or safe to grant at once to the Negro all the privileges which we ourselves have acquired by long struggles. History teaches us what terrible reactions have followed too extensive and too rapid changes."

Lincoln himself wrote to the Governor of Louisiana, Michael Hahn: "I barely suggest, for your private consideration, whether some of the colored people may not be let in, as for instance, the very intelligent, and especially those who have fought gallantly in our ranks. They would probably help, in some trying time to come, to keep the jewel of liberty within the family of freedom. But this is only a suggestion, not to the public, but to you alone."

With the assassination of Lincoln in 1865, however, the hopes of a nation for an easy return to normal were dashed. Thaddeus Stevens, a Radical Republican, for example, demanded that the property of rich rebels be confiscated, that Southern whites be disenfranchised and that the South be considered a conquered nation. "Settle the Southern states with new men," he said, "and exterminate or drive out the present rebels as exiles."

In fact, in 1867 a harsh Reconstruction Act divided the entire South into five military districts. At the same time, the Fourteenth Amendment to the United States Constitution gave the franchise to the Blacks. In 1868, General Ulysses S. Grant was elected President of the United States by a Negro majority of 700,000 votes.

Soon, at the urging of Northern politicians, New Orleans was filling up with carpetbaggers, that peculiar form of politician who had one goal and one goal only, and that was to get rich quick. They assumed public office and levied exorbitant taxes on everyone but themselves. They were corrupt, greedy and selfish. The governor of Louisiana, Henry Clay Warmoth, a carpetbagger himself, declared: "I do not pretend to be honest, only as honest as anybody in politics."

In addition to the carpetbaggers, Louisiana and the other Southern states were now governed by black men who had attained prominent places in the legislature, and scalawags – white Southern men who were attracted to the potential wealth of government. All, save the black men, were hungry to eat the fruits of a plundered South.

Between 1868 and 1875, these crooked politicians tripled the state's debt to over fifty million dollars and increased the taxes to such an extent that they could not be paid. The sheriff seized over 47,000 properties between 1871 and 1873 for unpaid taxes.

It was a hard time for New Orleans. Food was scarce and bitterness abundant. A Northern reporter wrote: "For breakfast there was salt fish, fried potatoes and treason. Fried potatoes, treason and salt fish for dinner and for supper, treason, salt fish, fried potatoes." A popular song ended:

"I can't take up my musket;
And fight 'em now no mo';
But I ain't gonna love 'em;
And that is sartain sho';
And I don't want no pardon;
For what I was and am;
And I won't be reconstructed;
And I don't care a damn."

Nevertheless, Louisiana and New Orleans in

particular, emerged from this period with more of a sense of racial equality than any other Southern state. As early as 1868, the Louisiana constitution forbade segregation in schools. In New Orleans there was such a concerted effort to mix the races that almost one third of the schools were integrated.

General Beauregard even established a new political party based on equality. He called it the Louisiana Unification Movement. It condemned segregation in places of public resort and public conveyances; asked for admission of all Blacks to schools on an equal basis; forbade employers to make a racial distinction when hiring, and asked that black stockholders be allowed to sit on boards of directors.

These projected policies were the result of radically different views from those widely held before the war. Nonetheless, the movement gained the support of many wealthy planters, the entire business community of New Orleans, the Catholic Church and the newspapers. It did not, however, win the support of the masses. Beauregard failed in his effort just as similar efforts failed in other states.

Finally, in 1877, Louisiana was readmitted to the Union. The next year Federal troops were withdrawn and the state began true recovery under self-government.

In the post-war era New Orleans needed its diversions. Voodoo was one of them. Voodoo seems to have arrived in New Orleans with the migration from Saint-Domingue of 10,000 black slaves following the bloody slave insurrections in 1809. The practice probably reached its height from 1850 to 1875. That was the time that Marie Laveau reigned as the "Voodoo Queen." During this time she was similarly known as "The Boss Woman of New Orleans."

The voodoo that Marie Laveau practiced was African in origin and combined touches of Catholicism, witchcraft and animism. She put on elaborate public spectacles to which she invited politicians, business leaders and the press. These unusual orgies, in which she often killed roosters, drank their blood and danced wild, uncontrolled dances with bamboula men and her venomous snake, were probably mostly for effect. Her most lucrative profession was as a peddler of information or, more likely, through blackmail for not peddling information. Her spy system included butlers, maids, hairdressers and cooks. Marie seems to have had something on almost everyone. She charged ten dollars to any superstitious person who wanted to get a lover or to get rid of one. If she was asked to put a hex on a politician for an opponent, she charged a

bit more.

Midway through her career she seemed to have gradually added more Roman-Catholic touches, so that incense, candles, statues and holy water became common. At the same time, she gave up the roosters, and even her huge, venomous snake. Although it is impossible to say that she conjured, hexed, told fortunes and placed or removed curses through love of God, at least it was slightly less sinister. She built a reputation for attending to the sick and those in prisons.

However, the formal practice of voodoo had virtually disappeared by the turn of the century. Nevertheless, it is not all that unusual for the local newspapers to report finding the requisite paraphernalia in one of the cemeteries, even today. It is unlikely, however, that a visitor to New Orleans would actually see a ceremony or even so much as a gris-gris.

A gris-gris is a charm, conjured up either for good or bad luck. It might take the form of colored pebbles, ground pepper and bits of bone, or it might be made of alligator entrails and herbs. A gris-gris might be worn in a bag around the neck or placed on a doorknob.

Nonetheless, it is still possible to buy some weird and unusual charms, amulets, dolls and powders in old New Orleans. How about a Love Powder, or a Dice Special (possibly intended for gamblers) or Come-to-Me Powder, or Luck-Around-Business Powder? Whether they work or not is probably more in the mind of the purchaser than in the force of the powder.

There is an interesting story though, of a man who was taking a trip from New Orleans to New York. His houseboy pleaded and pleaded to be allowed to accompany him. The man was firm in his opposition but, unaccountably, changed his mind a few days later and consented. Only years later did the houseboy confess that he had slipped some Boss Fix Powder into his food …

The end of Reconstruction saw another migration of immigrants. This time they were from Italy. It was not long after, probably about 1878, that the Mafia first arrived. It flourished. When they assassinated the New Orleans Chief of Police, the trouble was only just beginning. It did not take the police long to ferret out the killers. They soon arrested twenty-one members of the Matranga family. Although the evidence seemed conclusively to prove their guilt, the jury acquitted the lot.

Fury rose in New Orleans over the charge of jury tampering. The citizens decided it was time to take matters into their own hands. An angry mob proclaimed: "When the machinery of justice breaks down, the power to try and to execute criminals reverts to the people." In March, 1891, they broke into the jail and executed the Matranga gang. This harsh action was applauded by most New Orleans residents but, to avoid an international incident, the United States government apologized to Italy, paying a sum of $25,000.

Italian immigrants continued to pour into New Orleans. By 1910 they comprised nearly one third of the population. They were mostly farmers who grew string beans, beets, garlic, peppers, cabbage and turnips. Sicilians introduced the eggplant to New Orleans agriculture. They brought their produce to the old French Market for sale.

Creole families had been moving away from the French Quarter for some time. They rather liked the example set by the Americans in the Garden District, living in houses with a yard and flowers. The Italians moved into the vacated houses of the French Quarter.

Fortunately, they had little money to remodel and left the grand interiors largely as they found them. Life, indeed, was hard for the Italians, especially after the Mafia incident. They were not warmly received, but as their hard-working habits were recognized, they were assimilated into New Orleans culture.

Two Italian immigrants in particular made hard work pay dividends. Vincent Taormina arrived in New Orleans in 1900. He noticed how desperate Italians were for good Italian olive oil so he started importing it, and soon he expanded his line to include the importation of tomato products and other Italian specialties.

At the same time, the Uddo brothers had started operating their own truck farm. They also brought their produce to the French Market to sell. In 1928, the Taorminas and the Uddos joined forces. The company they founded is now known as Progresso Foods. Today they are manufacturers – the leading manufacturers of authentic quality Italian foods. The company is now so large that they process over twenty-five million pounds of tomatoes annually – a true success story!

To all nationalities, regardless of origin, entertainment was always top priority, and of all forms of entertainment Mardi Gras was the best – but even Mardi Gras suffered during the Civil War and Reconstruction. Folks tried to maintain the tradition but, in 1861, the first year of the war, floats were abandoned and marchers had to resort to foot. There were no parades again until 1866. However Mardi Gras did recover quickly.

1872 was an important year. His Imperial Highness, Alexis Alexandrovitch Romanoff of Russia was touring the United States. In New York he had seen a performance of *Bluebeard* starring the lovely *chanteuse*, Lydia Thompson. He fell in love and decided to follow her to New Orleans. He did not like people making a fuss over him, so he only told the newspapers, the Mayor and anyone else who would listen, that he would be stopping over in New Orleans for Mardi Gras. Actually, since he was traveling with three ships of the Imperial Russian Navy, it was difficult to keep it a secret.

No ordinary parade and celebration would do for a Grand Duke. But what could New Orleans do that was really special? They finally decided that they would create a ruler-king who would be the king of all carnival kings to be called "Rex."

The music took a new turn that year too. The Grand Duke not only fell in love with Lydia, but with a song she had sung. It was a silly little ditty, but perfectly suited to the revelry and fun of Mardi Gras. It became the theme of the 1872 Mardi Gras and has been the official song ever since. It is called *If Ever I Cease to Love*:

"If ever I cease to love,
May sheeps heads grow on apple trees
May the moon be turned into green cheese
May oysters have legs and cows lay eggs
If ever I cease to love ..."

The parade that year was an explosion of noise, color and music as over 5,000 marchers frolicked down the streets. They even had a huge, gaily decorated decoy bull, recruited from the stockyards to serve as the *Beouf Gras*. The Grand Duke loved it. He loved it so much that he stayed and stayed, falling in love with one actress after another.

The carpetbagger government during Reconstruction had horrible, debilitating effects on the economy of New Orleans. Everyone felt them. In 1873, the Comus parade undertook to voice criticism in the loudest and most humorous manner. They staged perhaps the most famous parade of all. The parade's title was "The Missing Links to Darwin's *Origin of the Species*." It was really just an excuse to portray various carpetbaggers, scalawags and other hated Yankees as half-animal creatures that had never quite made it through the evolutionary process. New Orleans loved it.

1873 was another important year too, because that was the first year that Rex took a queen. She was, as it turned out, the only married woman to ever serve in that role, and she was selected at random. When asked to comment on her experience she is reputed to have said: "It wasn't my best dress."

From that time on Mardi Gras just went from

strength to strength. The theme for Mardi Gras 1884, for example, was "The Passions." The floats depicted Love, Jealousy, Revenge, Gluttony, Envy and so on. Imagination and skill were used to great effect in creating the elaborate floats and costumes. Of course, planning time is also vital. No sooner is one Mardi Gras finished than the plans and arrangements for the following year's parade are well under way.

The practice of throwing trinkets to the expectant crowds probably originated with the parade of 1871, when a masked "Santa Claus" tossed "gifts." During a parade, the shouts of "Throw me something, mister!" are deafening. Beads are often used, but the most popular "throw" did not come along until 1969, when a man by the name of H. Alvin Sharpe wrote a letter to the captain of the Rex organization telling him about an inexpensive doubloon he had invented. It was an instant success – made of lightweight aluminum and sailing through the air like a paper airplane. Moreover, they are very difficult to catch, making them just that much more prized. Best of all, these doubloons are individualized according to each organization's specifications. One side bears the symbol for that year's parade and the other side bears a symbol of the krewe.

For New Orleans high society, the spirit of Mardi Gras consists in the elaborate masked balls. Local debutantes serve as queens – and invitations, especially to the three functions that are considered most "blue-blood" of all, are very scarce. It is to be esteemed a great honor to be invited to one of the events staged by the old families, old society and old money of New Orleans.

Even with all the hoopla and revelry connected with Mardi Gras, over the years some of the businessmen became concerned that it was not attracting enough tourists – surrounding all the gentility associated with society balls were solid entrepreneurs who were hoping to bring more business to New Orleans. If interest in Mardi Gras was clearly slacking the question was obviously what could be done to revitalize interest.

There seemed to be nothing for it but to introduce a whole new element, which is exactly what happened in 1969 – a tradition-breaking year. Those astute businessmen created a new parade, and what could be a more appropriate theme of revelry than a Bacchanalia? The 1969 parade was, therefore, called the Bacchus Parade and, to really liven things up, they asked a celebrity to be king. The first king was Danny Kaye and he played his role with characteristic gusto.

Floats for Bacchus are sometimes as many as two stories high – another first for Mardi Gras. As if that were not enough, instead of holding a grand by-invitation-only ball at the end of the festivities, they held a supper dance, open to all who wanted to pay the admission price. The whole idea was a resounding success. Other celebrities who have served as king of Bacchus include Bob Hope, Phil Harris, Pete Fountain, Glen Campbell and Henry Winkler.

Today's Mardi Gras is clearly not a substitute for the old *carnem levare*. There is not even a pretense that atonement for sins is the object. Besides, austere Lent follows on its heels anyway. It is a wonderful, joyous period of merriment – in a tradition unlike any other in the world. It has even been said that "Life starts after Mardi Gras."

Mardi Gras is not all that happens in New Orleans. It has always been a fairly wide-open town, but when Alderman Sidney Story sponsored legislation in 1897 to create a special district for pursuance of prostitution, the world's oldest profession really flourished. The area he designated was adjacent to the French Quarter and called Storyville. What a tribute to Alderman Story …

Basin Street was the most lavish of Storyville's streets. One could count thirty-five splendid mansions lining both sides of it. These palaces were hung with gaudy tapestries, decorated with crimson-plush upholstered furniture, and accessories that included gilt statuary, cut-glass chandeliers, leopardskin rugs and palm trees.

The queen of Storyville was Lulu White, and she ran the most lavish palace in town. She seems to have been extremely partial to diamonds as she wore diamond earrings, bracelets, necklaces, rings and even had a special set of diamond-encrusted teeth made to assure a dazzling smile. Her house had five elaborately decorated parlors and fifteen bedrooms.

Just a little further down Basin Street was the king of Storyville, a man by the name of Tom Anderson. He ran the Fair Play Saloon. This self-styled Mayor of Storyville actually won a seat in the state legislature and served for eight years. Next door to him was Josie Arlington's fantastic four-storied mansion.

Storyville had its own magazine, the *Blue Book* that described all the ladies of the night in vivid detail. Guests to the district would study the book to select their "hostess" for the evening. The *Blue Book* described Josie Arlington's palace as "absolutely and unquestionably the most decorative and costly fitted-out sporting palace ever placed before the American public." Of course, it is advisable to remember that the establishment placed its own advertisements.

Awe-struck tourists flocked to Storyville. They gaped in wonder at the lurid palaces dedicated to sin. At the height of its success, from 1897 to 1917, Storyville included 250 houses and about 2,000 girls. Not all of the girls were housed in elaborate mansions. On the back and side streets were little booths containing merely a table, a bed and a chair. These were called "cribs," and this section often exhibited a *joie de vivre* that the more elaborate places could not match. Women with long, black gloves, mesh stockings and "beauty spots" could be seen beckoning and calling to passers-by from their dimly lighted cribs. There could be nothing bashful or coquettish about these girls.

Dance halls and saloons were interspersed with mansions, and it is said that jazz was born in Storyville during the era preceeding World War I.

Music had long been one of the great passions of New Orleans. The French Opera Company opened its doors here in the mid-nineteenth century and had a long and highly successful career. It became the darling of New Orleans' high society from the day it opened. Tuesday and Saturday nights were the special province of New Orlean's élite, but on Sunday nights black people were welcomed. Singing stars such as Adelina Patti sang with them, and the company performed all the best-loved, famous operas. New Orleans even became the site of several American debuts of French operas. Sadly, the Opera House burned to the ground in 1919.

The St. Charles Theatre also brought famous musicians to New Orleans. For example, Violinists Ole Bull and the Frenchman Vieuxtemps both performed in New Orleans – on one occasion at least they were in New Orleans at the same time. P.T. Barnum brought Jenny Lind here on her American concert tour, and she stayed for a month. Tickets to her first concert were auctioned to the highest bidder. The first went for the fantastic price of $240. Lola Montez held concerts here too.

Louis Moreau Gottschalk was born in New Orleans in 1829. He became one of America's foremost pianists and composers. He often drew on his childhood in New Orleans for ideas. His composition *Bamboula*, for example, was inspired by the Sunday afternoons he spent in Congo Square watching and listening to the Negroes dance and sing. He was a virtuoso pianist and it is said that few pianists since have been able to perform his pieces with the same flair and sensuality.

He had his first European tour at the age of sixteen and rapidly became the darling of Paris. The French especially loved *Bamboula*, and the French papers all sang his praises. He was obviously a highly inventive composer, trying all sorts of new approaches.

One especially amusing incident occurred on a tour of San Francisco. He had arranged Wagner's march from *Tannhauser* for fourteen pianos. At the last minute one of his pianists became sick. Gottschalk felt the arrangement just would not sound right with one less piano. He searched and searched but could not find a suitable replacement. The owner of the concert hall had been pestering him to use his son and, finally, Gottschalk agreed, but only on the proviso that the son would attend a full rehearsal. The boy assured Gottschalk that he did not need to, but eventually he consented. After the first few bars it was apparent that the son was terrible, but what could be done to improve his playing at this late stage? Gottschalk's piano tuner came up with the solution. He removed the hammers, rendering the boy's piano mute.

The son had invited all his friends and strode on stage, resplendent in black tie and tails, bowing profusely first to one side and then the other. He performed superbly, so he thought, with all the embellishments befitting a virtuoso.

The evening was such a success that the pianists were urged back for an encore and the concert hall owner's son could not resist a short crescendo of his own, but no sound issued forth. Gottschalk saved the evening, and the boy's reputation, by beginning the encore. A performer to the end, the son apparently continued to contribute all his customary, mute embellishments, and perhaps no one suspected.

It is said that jazz was not invented, it just happened, and that it has its roots in the music played in Congo Square, at funerals, parades, band concerts, revival hymns, plantation spirituals, blues ballads, minstrel songs, ragtime, European folk music and street cries, as well as back rooms and bordellos. Willie Piazza, one of Storyville's mansion owners, loved good music. She employed a talented piano player – a man called Jelly Roll Morton – who alternately claims to have invented ragtime and jazz. Whatever the case, everyone loved his music. Jazz is characteristically American – sassy and cool – and it presented a perfect musical medium for laughing and crying about the peculiarities of the world.

The term "jazz" may have originated with the Afican word *jasi*, meaning "to act out of the ordinary." The New Orleans Jazz Museum says jazz is basically "any music played in two/four or four/four syncopated time by two or more tonal instruments improvising collectively." There is certainly no doubt that New Orleans jazz has a big, brassy sound and a pulsing beat.

The growth of jazz in New Orleans can best be viewed through the life of one of its greatest musicians. Louis Armstrong was born on the July 4th, 1900. At the age of six he started dancing and singing in the French Quarter for pennies. At thirteen he was sent to live in the Waif's Home. Fortunately, the home needed a trumpet player for their flag raising and lowering ceremonies, and Louis volunteered.

As his expertise grew, Louis played on riverboats and in mansions. Eventually, he moved to Chicago with King Oliver's Creole Jazz Band in 1922, and toured the world over, always to astounding popular acclaim. One of the greatest contributions to jazz musicianship was his ability to "cry up" to a note instead of hitting it straight on. He was the recognized "King of Jazz" and he brought a new understanding of this music form to the world. Always true to his home town, among his many honors was his election, in 1949, to be the Mardi Gras' King Zulu.

However, the credit for widely popularizing jazz probably belongs to a group of white New Orleans men. In 1914, Nick La Rocca formed the Original Dixieland Jazz Band. What made them different was that they recorded their sound on a new black disc, called a phonograph record, and sold many copies. Then they toured the United States, making jazz the national dance music.

Other early jazz greats included New Orleans musicians: Buddy Bolden, Bunk Johnson, Kid Ory and Sidney Bechet. All brought their own style to jazz and molded it into the great musical form that we know today. They were followed by Louis Armstrong, Pete Fountain, Woody Herman and Al Hirt.

It is easy to look back to those great days of Bourbon Street, when crowds thronged the streets trying to get into such places as Preservation Hall, Economy Hall and Funky Butt Hall. In these places the sounds would roll. When the tinkly sound of the piano would blend with the heavy beat of the drums; the blare of the trumpet with the mellow soft tones of the saxophone, underpinned by the throbbing beat of the double bass. That was jazz.

Sadly, the greats are gone now from Bourbon Street. Pete Fountain, the legendary clarinetist, who had his own lounge on Bourbon Street, has closed it and moved to the New Orleans Hilton. Woody Herman moved on too. Most recently the last remaining jazz star, Al Hirt, closed his club too. He claimed that he just could not make a profit and said: "I prefer to be in my own hometown. I love New Orleans. It's the place I was born. It's the place I love to live in. But I'm not going to work under those conditions." He does plan to reopen for the Louisiana World Exposition in 1984, however. Only

Preservation Hall continues to pack them in as regularly as it used to.

To look for such concessions as air conditioning, chairs or drinks in Preservation Hall is to be disappointed. For the most part Preservation Hall is a bare room filled to the rafters with music, and that is the fun of it. One can walk in anytime from eight o'clock in the evening to half past midnight, for an unbelievably low price, and listen to toe-tapping, ceaseless, jazz. Perhaps one may never be sure who is performing until you get there, but you will not be disappointed.

The corner of St. Peter and Bourbon streets might well be the "jazziest" corner in the world. There a visitor can find Maison Bourbon on one corner, Crazy Shirley's on another and, nearby, the Paddock and Famous Door. All still carry on the New Orleans jazz tradition. Later on at night is a good time to wander up to Funky Butts where the jazz greats gather for a late-night jam session.

Although not strictly jazz, Pat O'Brien's is certainly one of the liveliest places in town. It is a huge barn of a place, with one of the most beautiful patios in New Orleans. In the entertainment lounge just off the main entrance one will usually find two ladies playing twin pianos. They take requests, but the fun begins when a sing-along develops. That seems to be what the people enjoy the most. O'Brien's is a fun-filled, rollicking place, also known for its enormous "Hurricane" drinks and the special glasses in which they are served. Moreover, a guest is free to carry his or her drink right out onto the sidewalk, and it is not at all unusual to see folks sauntering over to Preservation Hall with drinks from Pat O'Brien's.

Jazz and drinking establishments certainly are not the only reasons to come to the French Quarter. It is also the heart and soul of New Orleans. In fact, Louise Pontalba is about to start one of her famous walking tours and she has invited us to join her so off we go:

We're starting our tour in Jackson Square. It is the square mentioned earlier that was originally called the Place d'Armes. It is the first section of the city that Bienville laid out and it borders on the river and we are going to walk to the riverside first. Simply turn around at this point and you can see the Square in all its glory.

In the middle a statue of General Jackson is mounted on a bronze horse. Louise tells us that the sculptor was Clark Mills and it was cast in 1856 at a cost of $30,000. It is really a very pleasing statue, somehow achieving a perfect balance in the posture of the horse and rider. She goes on to explain about an inscription on the base of the statue, which states:

"The Union Must and Shall be Preserved" – not exactly what one would expect from the hero of the Battle of Chalmette. He undoubtedly would have been a staunch Confederate had he lived. In fact, the inscription was added to the statue by "Beast" Butler during the Union occupation. One of his many insults to New Orleans.

Jackson Square had been the scene of many historical events. It started as a parade ground and, at one time, had even been used for public hangings, but Baroness de Pontalba (no relation to Louise) was successful in having it transformed into a garden in 1856. We will hear more about the Baroness later. Today, Jackson Square is a lovely oasis along the lines of a public patio or courtyard. It is surrounded, except along the riverside, by magnificent historic buildings.

Just behind the statue of General Jackson, for example, is St. Louis Cathedral. Louise tell us this is actually the third St. Louis church on this site. The first was destroyed in a hurricane in 1723. The second burned to the ground in the infamous fire of 1788. The present building was erected in 1794 and was almost entirely financed by Don Andres Almonester y Roxas, a wealthy Spanish nobleman. A marble slab marks his grave under the altar. It has been remodeled several times over the years, so this is not the original design. Nevertheless, it is truly lovely. Worthy of notice the high central tower with the two lower towers at each end.

Let us go inside for a moment. The six stained-glass windows, donated by Spain, in 1962 are very special. They depict scenes from the period when New Orleans was under Spanish domination. Moreover, be sure to stand for a moment and study the magnificent painting above and behind the altar. The figure is Louis IX sending his men off on the Seventh Crusade from the steps of Notre Dame.

Back out in Jackson Square, Louise is taking us to the Cabildo next, which is that rather severe building just to the right as we leave the Cathedral. Louise tells us that it is an excellent example of Hispano-Mooresque architecture, identifiable by its wide arches. The French added its mansard roof, though, in 1847. The building was erected by the Spanish as their seat of government, and has been used by succeeding governments as well.

It was in the Cabildo that the official transfer of the Louisiana Territory from France to the United States took place, and it has been the place where honored guests were officially welcomed to New Orleans. When Lafayette visited New Orleans in 1825, for example, he was received at the Cabildo. Others who have been received here include the Grand

Duke Alexis of Russia, Mark Twain, Presidents Theodore Roosevelt, William McKinley and William Howard Taft, as well as Sarah Bernhardt and Henry Clay.

The Cabildo is now home to the Louisiana State Museum and well worth a visit. Napoleon's death mask (donated by his personal physician who later came to live in New Orleans) is on display there. Moreover, there is an art gallery on the second floor, and the Mississippi River exhibition, detailing the development of plantations and riverboats, is also fascinating.

From the moment we entered the Square, it has been hard to take our eyes off those lovely, symmetrical, four-story, red-brick buildings with their elegant cast-iron balcony railings, which line St. Peter and St. Ann streets along Jackson Square. Louise informs us they are known as the Pontalba Buildings (again no relation, but she still exhibits a characteristic pride). They were built by Micaela Almonester Pontalba, the daughter of Don Almonester, the financier of St. Louis Cathedral. She completed the sixteen rows of houses on St. Peter Street in 1850. It is believed they were the first apartment houses in the United States. The houses on St. Ann Street were finished the following year, and they still retain their wonderful, small, ground-level shops. The apartments above are enormous and have high windows and high ceilings, making them light and airy. They all have access to the balcony. If you look closely at the beautiful cast-iron balcony railing, you may see the intertwined initials A.P. They denote the Almonester and Pontalba families.

On the other side of St. Louis Cathedral. Louise points out the the Presbytère, saying that it was originally intended as a residence for the Cathedral priests. It looks a lot like the Cabildo, but this building is two stories high and built of stuccoed brick. This, too, is a branch of the Louisiana State Museum.

What is that strange object over there under the colonnade? Louise explains that it is the first iron submarine ever made. The Confederate Navy thought they had the ultimate weapon. It was launched in 1861 and could travel all of four miles an hour. The Union soldiers were too swift for the Confederates, though. Even before the submarine could be used, New Orleans was an occupied city, so the Navy sunk the submarine in Lake Pontchartrain to avoid its capture.

From this point we are moving briskly down to the old French Market. Louise tells us there has been a market here since the Choctaw Indians first traded with the French. The first buildings were built by the

Spanish in 1791, but the present buildings probably date from 1813. It is a lively place, that is for sure. It seems to extend for about six blocks and is an ideal place to watch people!

In fact, Louise is giving us forty-five minutes to do just as we please. There are a great deal of souvenir shops mixed in with the stalls bearing fruits and vegetables, fish and meat. It is a great place to buy some typical Creole candies, and pralines too. Probably the best thing to do for satiating a sweet tooth, however, is to take a seat at the famous Café du Monde.

New Orleans coffee is unlike any other. It is thick, strong and generally laced with chicory. It was hard to get coffee during the Civil War, you see, so ingenious New Orleans folk started substituting chicory. They generally drank it in the form of half hot milk and half coffee, and their *café au lait* is unlike any other. It is the speciality of the Café du Monde.

Nothing could be better, especially if it is accompanied by one or several steaming-hot beignets, those feathery light doughnuts, crisp on the outside and soft inside, that are sprinkled with powdered sugar. They are a typical New Orleans treat.

We are told that the Café du Monde and the other coffee houses scattered throughout the French Market are the perfect place to end an evening in New Orleans. They are romantic places and full of fun, and that coffee does taste good. Does it come in a decaffeinated form, I wonder? Louise does not know, but she does know our time for refreshment is up.

We are not far from the Ursuline Convent. This is probably the oldest structure in the Mississippi Valley, completed in 1745. The Ursuline nuns were the first to establish a school in the French colony and the first to establish an orphanage. They acted both as teachers and nurses.

Across the street is the Beauregard-Keyes House. General Beauregard lived here in a rented room while he was looking for work after the Civil War. It is a sad tale to hear about the once proud General, defeated by the war and penniless, reduced to living in a rented room.

This house is doubly famous because, from the mid 1950s to 1970, it served as the home of Frances Parkinson Keyes, a prolific novelist. Many of her stories revolved around New Orleans and the Deep South. Her novel *Madame Castel's Lodger* is about General Beauregard's stay in her house. Another of her novels, *Dinner at Antoine's*, celebrates the famous French Quarter restaurant of that name.

Since we are so close, we should wander over to Royal Street. Our goal is the Lalaurie house, the "haunted house" of the Quarter, at 1140 Royal Street. Louise tells us that Madame Lalaurie is supposed to have chained her servants in the attic and even tortured them. On one occasion a little Negro girl is supposed to have leaped from the roof to avoid the lashings. Apparently the moans can still be heard from the house on a quiet night.

We are going to walk down Rue Royale now. Take a look at the elaborate cornstalk fence outside the house at 915 Royal Street. It was brought to New Orleans in 1834 by a doctor whose wife missed the cornfields surrounding her former home in the midwest. It is one of the most photographed spots in the French Quarter. Notice the shucked ears intertwined with morning glory vines and blossoms. There is even a butterfly on the gate.

By the way, the streetcar named *Desire* once traveled this street. Tennessee Williams made it famous in his play of the same name. The original is now parked over at the Old Mint on Esplanade Street.

The LaBranche House, at 700 Royal Street, is not to be missed either. Have you ever seen so much lacy, iron grillwork? It is another photographer's dream. All three levels of the house fairly drip with entwined oak leaves and acorns.

Louise next escorts us down the street to Brennan's Restaurant at 417 Royal Street. It is reputed to be just about one of the greatest restaurants in New Orleans – perhaps the United States. It is found in a lovely old mansion that once served as a bank. Louise tells us that a meal in the cool courtyard, or on the upstairs balconies should not be missed – it is very romantic. There are flowers everywhere, a gentle breeze stirs the palm leaves and soft background music plays.

Brennan's is noted for its breakfasts as well as its dinners – and what breakfasts they are! You would not want to miss one. It could start off with a New Orleans Gin Fizz, maybe two, and then perhaps an order of their famous Eggs Sardou – poached eggs served on a bed of spinach and artichoke bottoms, topped with Hollandaise Sauce. Believe it or not, most folks would not miss the Bananas Foster for dessert either. It is made right at your table in a chafing dish. The banana and brown sugar are flamed with rum and banana liquor and served over vanilla ice cream. That and a cup of hot coffee will set you up for the day. You definitely will not go away hungry, Louise tells us, but it is wise to make reservations.

We are walking over to Bourbon Street now, where all the old jazz clubs used to be. Down just two blocks from Canal Street, at 238 Bourbon, is the Old Absinthe House. It was named for a very potent drink that later turned out to be narcotic. The drink has been outlawed for some time now, but that does not mean they do not still serve potent libations. The building has all sorts of legends associated with it.

There is a persistent rumor that General Andrew Jackson and Jean Lafitte planned the defense of New Orleans from a tiny second floor room here. Take a look at the hundreds and hundreds of calling cards papering the walls. During Prohibition it was a speak-easy. Then it was closed down in 1924 by the revenuers. All the fixtures, including the long marble bar, were moved up to 400 Bourbon Street. Actually, the Brennan family, who own Brennan's Restaurant, were responsible for restoring this place. It became such a goldmine that they decided to open their full-fledged restaurant as well.

There is so much more to see in the French Quarter, but Louise tells us that it is best to just wander around on foot alone and take it all in. There are homes with original furnishings open to the public and another chance unfolds to go back and see the Cabildo and Presbytère, or to see the exhibits at the Louisiana State Museum. Louise has another tour to lead right now though, so we bid her farewell.

Before Louise left she suggested that we might want to take a walk over to see St. Louis Cemetery No. 1. These burial grounds are called "Cities of the Dead" in New Orleans and they are unlike cemeteries anywhere else.

New Orleans' ground is so soggy and damp that burying corpses underground was simply impractical in the early days. There are stories about gravediggers needing to bail all the water out of the hole they had dug only minutes before placing the coffin inside. People had nightmares about coffins floating away in the middle of the night. However, New Orleans ingenuity prevailed again.

They decided that the only solution was to bury the dead above ground. So they built brick tombs, faced with plaster. There is usually a door in front with an inscription on a marble tablet. Some are even surrounded by cast-iron fences. All are neatly arranged along narrow paths, for all the world like cities. Some of the paths even have street names. Some of the tombs are more grand than others, of course. There are skyscrapers and Italianate villas and Georgian columns and roofs with eaves. The poor are buried in ovens along the outside walls. It is fascinating to read the inscriptions. They speak tellingly about every yellow fever epidemic (and there were many) and about family life. Marie Laveau, the Voodoo Queen, is buried in St. Louis No. 1, and it is said that, even to this day, a gris-gris that is left at her tomb overnight is sure to have an influence the next day.

An important part of any visit to New Orleans is its food, and New Orleans cuisine plays a great part of the life of the folks who live here too. Blessed with an abundance of fresh fish and shellfish from the sea; a long growing season on the land and an exotic blend of cuisines and customs, New Orleans cuisine consists of a wonderful mélange of styles. There is something for every appetite and palate. Cajun food is hot and spicy, Creole food is a more subtle blend of Spanish and French traditions. Also part of the New Orleans culinary tradition is the cuisine brought from Africa by the Negro slaves, who became cooks on the large plantations, as well as the Indians, who were there in the first place. Then there are the more recent additions of Italian and German cooking. New Orleans cooking offers the full range of all the traditions of the various nationalities that make up the city.

New Orleans cuisine started to develop some of its unique characteristics with the arrival and influence of the first French settlers. Those wonderful French cooks simply did not have the right ingredients to make the bouillabaisse, or the breads they had made at home, so they started improvising. They learned from the Indians how to make bread with cornmeal and how to pound the dried leaves of the sassafras tree into a powder that imparts a delicate flavor, almost like that of thyme, and is even good for thickening stock. When the Acadians arrived, they taught the old-timers all sorts of new things. Like how to use shellfish and local fish in the bouillabaise. They still made some of those delicate French dishes with lovely sauces, but they added new ingredients to them and they started making up new dishes altogether.

The traditional French bouillabaise would have used lobsters, eels, three kinds of white fish (perhaps from a selection of halibut, red snapper, bass, haddock, pollack, hake, cod, yellow pike, lake trout, whitefish or rockfish), mussels and sea scallops, as well as leeks, tomatoes, fennel, garlic, thyme, saffron, bay leaf, green pepper, chili pepper, pimentos, cloves etcetera. Most of these ingredients were simply unattainable in New Orleans.

What they improvised evolved as a typical New Orleans dish called gumbo. It may have as its base a combination of crab, shrimp or oysters, or it may use duck and sausage or even squirrel and oysters. Just about anything that is near at hand at the time might go in. In addition, though, you might often find okra – the basic ingredient that came from Africa and is used to thicken the gumbo – as well as chili, Tabasco and a bit of cayenne. The original French fish soup has now been transformed into a thick Creole/

Acadian stew – a good example of ingenuity.

Part of the reason for the spicy pungency of New Orleans cooking is the abundance of that unusual and very hot pepper that is processed in Tabasco sauce. These hot little peppers are grown on a tiny island 125 miles west of New Orleans, called Avery Island. It is really more of a hill that rises 150 feet above the low-lying swamps and bayous.

Avery Island's base is pure salt and its surface is pure pepper. Folks learned the secret of Tabasco sauce about one hundred years ago when the seeds were imported from Mexico, and have been fond of it ever since. Avery Island grows a great deal of peppers, and every drop of the Tabasco brand sauce the world over comes from right here.

Making Tabasco sauce is not an easy process, though. Only the reddest peppers are picked by hand in the fall. They are then doused with salt from the base of the hill and mashed to a pulp. The mash is placed in large oak barrels, more salt is sprinkled on top and they are covered with a perforated lid. This keeps the air out but allows gas to escape. The mash is left in the barrels to ferment for three years.

When the casks are opened the fermented mash is mixed with vinegar and churned for thirty days. Then it is just about ready, but for a few more steps, including straining, filtering and bottling. Over ten million bottles of Tabasco Brand pepper sauce are shipped by the McIlhenny Company from Avery Island every year to such exotic places as Australia and Zaire, Madagascar and Hong Kong. Indeed, what would a Bloody Mary be without a touch of Tabasco?

What would New Orleans be without oysters? One of the most popular local lunchtime treats is to sidle up to a popular oyster bar for some fresh-off-the-halfshell oysters. Most bars will offer you a paper cup in which to mix your own dipping sauce. Perhaps you might want tomato sauce with lemon or vinegar, a touch of Tabasco and a bit of horseradish. Or you might prefer just a little lemon juice and freshly ground pepper. Either way, you will probably need a good cold beer to wash it down.

Oyster farming is big business here. With all the oysters consumed, the industry needs a helping hand. It is a fascinating business. A female and a male oyster rarely even see one another. Each simply secretes a substance in the water and the sperm and eggs somehow find each other. A female will lay as many as sixty million eggs. Few of these will ever reach maturity. The baby oysters swim freely until they find a likely place to attach themselves. Male oysters attach themselves for life. Except that they change sex at least twice in their lifespan, but when they are male, they are attached, either to other oysters or to rocks.

It is this that an oyster farmer can take advantage of. A farmer will seed a bay bottom with thousands of discarded oyster shells. Young oysters like this bed the best of all and are attracted to it in their thousands. The farmer leaves them there for about a year and a half and then he rakes them up and take them to a saltier area where they will grow and mature. From that place they are taken out and go straight to market.

Louisiana crayfish (or crawfish or crawdaddy, as some call it – even *écrevisses* in French) is a delicacy that should not be missed, especially if one is in New Orleans from May to July – the crayfish season. They taste somewhat like lobsters, but generally they are only three to five inches long, and each crayfish weighs about one ounce. Some eighteen million pounds of crayfish are consumed annually.

Catching them is not at all easy however. They seem to love meat, so either a baited cage is lowered into a pond or they are caught individually by dangling a piece of meat from the end of a stick into the water. Sometimes the yield is worth all the work and sometimes it is not.

Crayfish is a typical Cajun specialty and harvesting them is often a family adventure. The larger the family the better. It is fairly common to see eighteen to twenty crayfish consumed at a sitting. Many have to be harvested in order to have any left over to take to market.

A typical Cajun way of serving crayfish would be to cook them in a peppery stew with rice; or serve them as a crayfish jambalaya; or, perhaps most likely, to boil them in a spicy broth and serve them out of the shell.

As long as I live I will never forget a memorable meal I once had in a New Orleans restaurant. At a table for six just off in a corner, sat a convivial group of obviously very knowledgeable people. The specialty of the evening was crayfish and the host was instructing his guests in the proper way to eat them. I remember he said to break the tail part in half and pull out the meat. Then he demonstrated how to suck out the last drop of juice from each of the shells – considered to be a great delicacy. All the guests wore bibs and they kept on ordering and reordering. Just to watch the proceedings was a treat.

Fish and shellfish are not the only specialties of New Orleans cuisine worth writing home about. There are the desserts too. One of the most famous and popular are the delicious candies called pralines, mentioned earlier in connection with the French Market. They are a confection made from sugar, butter and pecans, melted and swirled about in a heavy pot until they are golden colored.

For more formal meals, a good old New Orleans pecan pie just can not be beaten. Nothing could taste better at the end of a New Orleans meal than a hot piece of fresh pecan pie topped with a dollop of whipped cream or ice cream.

A good place to get a sampling of pralines, crayfish, oysters and gumbo would have been the Louisiana World Exposition, which took place in New Orleans from May to November, 1984. It is especially interesting to note that the Fair took place exactly one hundred years after the "World's Industrial and Cotton Centennial Exposition" in 1884.

That first one was held both to honor King Cotton and to bring new business to New Orleans, and it was certainly impressive. It was located on the site of Audubon Park and covered thirty-three acres. This one Fair used more elevators in one place than existed in the rest of the world; it had an exhibition hall that could seat 8,000 people and a music hall that could seat 11,000. Its pipe organ was the largest in North America, and electrical lighting was one of the wonders of the Cotton Centennial – the glass tower on the Horticultural Hall was lit up at night and could be seen as far away as twenty miles afield.

The Cotton Exposition was an extravaganza. In addition to the industrial and commercial exhibits displayed, there were on-site taverns and gambling houses. This was before the days of Storyville and a visitor had this to say: "Brilliantly lighted by a new electric-flare system, the street is thronged with men of all classes, who enter or emerge from its many saloons and gambling houses, which throb with the raucous sounds of pleasure-bent men and women. Timid crowds of men stand upon the curbstone to catch a glimpse of female limbs draped in gauze of pink and blue ... Arrayed in scant garments, but gorgeous in combinations of colors, are young and middle-aged; youthful and fresh, together with wearied and worn, whited sepulchers; watching among the throng which enters, those whom their judgment dictates have money to spend or throw away upon them in remuneration for a display of their utter unconsciousness of virtue."

The 1984 version may not have had the wide-open atmosphere of an Old-West town, but it exceeded the earlier Cotton Exposition in every other way. It covered an eighty-two-acre site just two blocks upriver from the Rivergate Exhibition Center, and its theme, appropriate in a city nurtured by the Mississippi, was "Rivers of the World – Fresh Water As a Source of Life."

Previous page: St. Louis Cathedral, its white walls golden by floodlight, rises beyond the bronze of General Jackson that stands in the center of Jackson Square in the Vieux Carré. Right: skyscrapers dwarf the stern-wheeler Natchez in uptown New Orleans. Crescent City, as New Orleans is nicknamed for its position on a sweeping curve on the Mississippi River (overleaf), was founded in 1718 and named for Philippe, Duke of Orléans, the powerful regent of Louis XV of France. The area was swampy, humid, mosquito-ridden and frequently flooded – hardly the ideal spot for any human habitation, let alone a city – but the site was strategically important since it commanded the mouth of this huge river. So arduous was the task of draining the ground that France had to ship out convicts to tackle it, there being no free men willing to do the work, and apparently even the prisoners – despite the severest of penalties – refused to co-operate on occasion.

These pages and overleaf: some of the imposing, plantation-style residences set beside the rows of live oaks – many of which are two hundred years old – that are characteristic of St. Charles Avenue, one of the city's most elegant thoroughfares in uptown New Orleans. Uptown – in other words "up river" – became, after the Louisiana Purchase by the United States in 1803, the commercial and residential center of business-like Anglo-Americans, and these are their houses. Downtown was, and remains, the old Franco-Spanish city known as the Vieux Carré.

A deepening blue sky and long shadows across the green herald the fall of evening in Jackson Square. This square centers upon a technically innovative equestrian bronze of General Jackson, the first in the world to have more than one hoof unsupported. Unveiled in 1856, the bronze was cast by Clark Mills and is reputedly a good likeness of the illustrious general and his spirited horse. Overleaf: the New Orleans waterfront. For all its concrete and steel frontage, the great Mississippi still has some choice spots for fishing and, in places, retains the air of a country backwater. Nevertheless, this river – the source of all New Orleans' prosperity – can be a dangerous neighbor. During periods of high water, the surface of the river may be ten to twenty feet above street level. Now it is prevented from inundating the city by a fortress of levees, but in 1965, when New Orleans was without a comprehensive network of embankments, Hurricane Betsy flooded the city's lower Ninth Ward.

Lafitte's Blacksmith Shop (facing page top) on Bourbon Street was owned by the pirate brothers,
Jean and Pierre Lafitte. It was rumored that the outlaw Frenchmen used the smithy as cover for
their illegal activities, secreting slaves and contraband there. Facing page bottom: Beauregard-
Keyes House on Chartres Street in the Vieux Carré, named for two famous occupants: the
Confederate general, Pierre Beauregard and the authoress Frances Parkinson Keyes. Above: Soniat
House on the same street, and (overleaf) a saxophonist busking below some of the spectacular
ironwork for which New Orleans architecture is renowned.

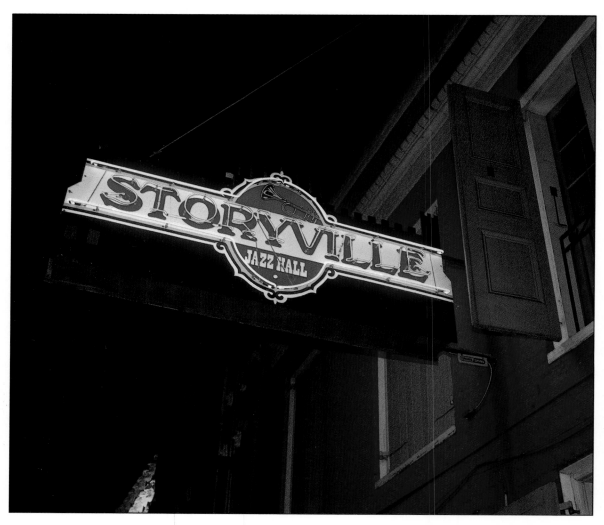

These pages: neon signs form an avenue of lights along the honky-tonk strip of the Rue Bourbon, designed to entice the night people in this "City that Care Forgot." Every third building along this street is a nightclub and the cabaret acts and strippers that parade inside them are world famous. Overleaf: New Orleans prepares to swelter through another tropical night. In the summer, the city temperature averages 91°F and thermometer readings of 100°F are not unusual.

These pages and overleaf: New Orleans musicians in a jam session. Jazz originated in New Orleans between the 1880s and the First World War and is proudly performed here in a wide variety of atmospheric bars and clubs dedicated to keeping authentic jazz alive. Every April this aim is highlighted when the city hosts an International Jazz and Heritage Festival comprising several weeks' celebration of ragtime, blues, gospel and Cajun music, as well as Dixieland jazz.

Above: a clarinetist and a trumpeter team up with a pianist in a jazz bar. Jazz originated from music played by slaves in the open air – a situation that may have accounted for the dominance of the trumpet, which, because of its strident tones, was used for the melody. Later, when jazz was more often heard in bars (these pages and overleaf), the piano would play the melody line, freeing the trumpet for spectacular flights of improvisation.

These pages: New Orleans street scenes. Here, in the home of improvised music, a busker is to be found at virtually every corner, so, be it inside the bars and clubs or outside in the street, New Orleans is always alive with some sort of rhythm and blues. Overleaf: Royal Street, the main thoroughfare of the Vieux Carré, where antique shops, art galleries and open air cafés proliferate and a sense of bygone romance beguiles the visitor. Royal Street was named for the groups of dispossessed aristocrats, exiled from France after the Revolution, who gathered in its cafés to plot their return to the Old Country.

Jackson Square seen from the air. It was around this square that the founder of New Orleans, Bienville – who had an auspicious name, as it turned out – directed engineers to lay the city out in 1718. He didn't spend long casting around for a suitable spot for the city center, since one part of a swamp looks much like another – Jackson Square was simply where he set foot ashore. For many years the square, known as the Place des Armes, was used as a parade ground, not only by the French, but by the Spanish and the Americans too – the flags of all three countries have flown above this green. Overleaf: the Louisiana Superdome, its distinctive shape setting it apart from its rectangular neighbors. Home of the New Orleans Saints, the Superdome is the world's largest enclosed stadium, covering fifty-two acres and reaching twenty-seven stories in height.

Loyola University, established by Jesuits in 1911, blazes forth on St. Charles Avenue. A castellated celebration of Gothic Revival architecture built in red brick and white stone, Loyola is the oldest Catholic university in the South and was named after the founder of the Jesuit Order, Ignatius Loyola. Overleaf: a bronze Andrew Jackson gallantly raises his cocked hat in the square that bears his name. Jackson became a hero of the city when he led American forces to a resounding victory against an invading British army in the Battle of New Orleans in January, 1815. Ironically, the battle was unnecessary since the War of 1812 was already over – the Treaty of Ghent having been signed between the United States and Britain in Europe on Christmas Eve, 1814. Sadly for those who died, however, news of this had not even reached the East Coast, let alone Louisiana, by January.

71

Spring softens the sober frontage of Tulane University, which was founded in 1834 as the Medical College of Louisiana and today incorporates a wide educational program, including a law department specializing in the Code Napoléon, the legal system exclusive, in the United States, to Louisiana. As a thriving educational center, New Orleans is the seat of four universities, a medical center, various colleges and several theological seminaries. Overleaf: the great Mississippi. "Ole Man River," its banks regimented into concrete wharfs and its waters tamed by levees, remains the lifeblood of New Orleans and her most timeless attraction.

A harmony of rich brown and dark gray roofs in the Vieux Carré, where the gardens are punctuated by shady trees and the courtyards and patios have been designed as external rooms to provide relief from the heat during the city's humid summer afternoons. The names of these narrow streets – Toulouse, Dumaine, Burgundy, Chartres and Bourbon – reveal their French origins, but visitors dutifully pronouncing them with a French accent will find that they are misunderstood by the locals. The Vieux Carré isn't a reproduction of Montmartre, for all its balconied houses, street cafés full of would-be writers and artists' sketches hanging on the railings of Jackson Square. This is a far more eclectic mix, boasting Creole, Cajun, African and Spanish cultures that have combined to form a heady atmosphere – and a distinctive "French" dialect – in one of the most exciting city centers in the New World.

Despite a plethora of cast-iron columns that could serve the purpose, a horse-head hitching post has been provided in this Vieux Carré street (above), and in New Orleans it is not yet an anachronism, since horse-drawn carriages (above right) still ply their trade, fringed and decked with flowers, to the delight of romantics. Right and overleaf: New Orleans street cars – none of which is named "Desire", although the Desire line did exist, passing Le Monnier House where Tennessee Williams, author of the famous play A Streetcar Named Desire, once lived. Today only the St. Charles Avenue line remains, the last of a network that dated from the 'Twenties.

Left: unlike a his colleagues in less relaxed cities, a New Orleans cab driver can stretch out in the sun as he awaits his next fare, his satin top hat glistening beside the shiny paintwork of his carriage, while (above) office workers take the St. Charles line to uptown New Orleans. The cabs and the street cars of this city lend particular neighborhoods considerable nostalgic charm. Overleaf: twilight in Audubon Park, named for the French artist John James Audubon, who taught drawing in New Orleans. The park, developed from a sugar plantation in the 1870s, is large enough to accommodate a zoo, an open-air theater, a botanical garden and, appropriately, a statue of Audubon.

These pages and overleaf: the well-preserved stern-wheeler Natchez – like the street cars and the horse-drawn carriages, one of the historic means of transport that this sentimental city refuses to discard. In their heyday, before the Civil War, individual steamboats didn't last many years since their boilers were prone to explode, a tendency exacerbated by the competitive spirit of the steamboat captains, who would often indulge in spontaneous races. Such practices were partly responsible for the 4,000 deaths that occurred in steamboat disasters between 1810 and 1850, yet such hazards deterred few. Within twenty years of the first stern-wheeler run in 1812 there were 1,200 such vessels carrying cotton, sugar and humankind along this mighty river. Indeed, until an improved rail network served a redundancy notice upon it in the 1870s, the steamboat was the way to travel to New Orleans.

These pages: the Mardi Gras volcano blows and once again a joyous lava of people fills the streets of New Orleans as an army of tractors haul some of the world's finest carnival floats (overleaf) into view. A traditional pre-Lenten celebration, the Mardi Gras is more elaborately celebrated here than anywhere else in the country for none know how to enjoy themselves better than the cosmopolitan population of New Orleans.

Legend has it that once, in a Mardi Gras parade, a woman participant found her rope of seed pearls too constricting, so she took them off and – in a splendidly careless gesture typical of the spirit of carnival – flung them into the crowd. Since then, each parade group (these pages) – known as a krewe – hurls thousands of glass necklaces, trinkets and doubloons into the outstretched hands of the crowd (overleaf) in celebration of her spontaneous example.

These pages: Mardi Gras revelers don masks, grease paint and the most unlikely costumes and take to the streets – and the balconies – in joyous celebration. The Mardi Gras is a chance for everybody to lose themselves behind a colorful disguise and enjoy a new persona. Visitors to the city at this time are enjoined to wear a mask at the very least and, given the general tendency towards fancy dress, many do, and dignity is put aside for the day. Mardi Gras crowds (overleaf) can swell to a million and a half.

Right: sleek mules doze beside Jackson Square (overleaf), the lacy iron railings of one the Pontalba Buildings forming the backdrop to their siesta. Considering the care she lavished upon their construction, it is apt that these buildings are named for the woman who built them, Micaela Almonester de Pontalba. During the 1840s, Micaela, an extremely wealthy baroness, commissioned the finest architects of the city to build these apartments, personally supervised the demolition of the previous structures on the sites, ordered all the building materials herself and added her own touches to the design when she felt so inclined. Ever a woman ready to get involved, she thought nothing of flouting the conventions of the day by donning pantaloons to ascend ladders to inspect her workmen's efforts. The apartments, which flank the right and the left sides of Jackson Square, were the first of their kind in the country; today they are owned by the city and the Louisiana State Museum.

These pages: the Hermann-Grima House, which, with its Georgian architecture, is unique in the Vieux Carré. Creole houses usually have discreetly shuttered doors, rear porte-cochère entrances and, inside, rooms open onto one another directly from the porte-cochère. In contrast, Samuel Hermann's house, built in 1831 on Saint Louis Street, faces the street, its formal doorways are flanked by tall sash windows (facing page) and it sports an elegant hall (top) — all features which must have given his guests pause.

These pages and overleaf: Oak Alley, probably the most famous of all Louisiana plantation homes, due to its superbly romantic setting at the end of an avenue of live oaks that leads down to the Mississippi. The oaks were already a century old when sugar planter Jacques Roman bought this site on the River Road in 1837 to construct a home for his bride. The mansion he built was originally called Bon Sejour, but its name was changed when passengers on Mississippi steamboats expressed so much interest in the distinctive quarter mile of trees leading to its doors.

Facing page: the McBertie House in early fall, where orange trees dip to the damp courtyard in the cool of the early morning, and (top) wood floors gleaming in one of the house's ground-floor rooms. The absence of carpets is a reflection of the New Orleans summer heat, which makes them redundant – the same principle holds true in Lupin House (above), another nineteenth-century residence, whose walls are hung with modern art.

Richly ornamented lampposts mark the entrance from Jackson Square into the Cabildo. During Spanish rule, this building housed the governing council, or cabildo, of the colony. As befits the importance of the building it graces, the wrought-iron balcony by Marcelino Hernández is considered to be the finest ironwork of the Spanish period in New Orleans. Inside the Cabildo, in a room known as the Sala Capitular, France ceded the territory of the Louisiana Purchase to the United States in 1803, after which Old Glory was flown for the first time from the superb balcony. From the same vantage point in 1815, Jefferson waved to a New Orleans crowd rejoicing at his victory over the British. Could he have guessed then that forty years in the future his statue would be unveiled in that same square in honor of his triumph?

Top: Hobson House shines by night, its elegant facade evoking those luxurious days when carriages would draw up in front of such palatial homes to shower forth silken-gowned Southern belles for summer balls. Above and facing page: richly decorated rooms in the Hermann-Grima House. Overleaf: sunset finds the keenest of yachtsmen still plying the waters of Lake Pontchartrain, the city's vast lake, which provides recreation for lovers of watersports. Three yacht clubs are based here, one of which – the Southern Yacht Club – is the country's second oldest.

INDEX